REFRAME
Foundations For Freedom And Fullness In Christ!

Clay & Laura Gatlin

Clay & Laura Gatlin
Reframe Ministries, Inc.
www.yourreframe.com

Print ISBN-13: 978-0-578-55623-9

Printed in the United States of America

Library of Congress Cataloging-in-Publication Data is on file at the Library of Congress, Washington, DC.

REFRAME

Foundations For Freedom And Fullness In Christ!

Scripture references are taken from the following and used by permission:

Acknowledgements

We are so grateful to those who have helped us take the transforming work of God in our lives and communicate it in written form. Special thanks to our Board of Directors (Bob, Cortland, D'Ette, Greg, Laura, Matt, Mindy, Scott) here at Reframe Ministries, Inc. Your love, encouragement, wise counsel, prayer support, and partnership makes this Kingdom work possible.

Special thanks to Cortland for the painstaking time spent making sure we stayed true to 2 Timothy 2:15 (ESV) - "Do your best to present yourself to God as one approved, a worker who has no need to be ashamed, rightly handling the Word of Truth." Thank you, Matt, for helping shape and make the book readable. We're also thankful to those who took the time to proof it and provided all the helpful feedback. Special thanks to our friends David & Karen (our earliest mentors) for the editorial help.

The final product of this book, ministry and ongoing church partnerships would never have been a reality without my good friend, Greg. Thank you for the overwhelming investment of your time, talent, and treasures!

Thank you, Bryan and Kelli (Clay's friends from childhood). You have walked faithfully and sacrificially with us over the years. We wouldn't quite be the same without your friendship!

We wouldn't have this testimony without all the churches we have served in and worked alongside. Through all the good experiences and painful challenges, we are grateful for how the Lord has worked all these out to accomplish His will.

To our family and friends, so much of our learning and growing has been at your expense. We can never repay you for the sacrifices you have made that have led to our freedom and fullness in Christ. We will always remember your investment and sacrifice, and we commit to steward it well. To Clay's parents, thank you for the partnership, example, sacrifice, and support from the very beginning! To Laura's parents, thank you for always believing in us and loving us through all the crazy season in our lives.

Preface

First of all, thank you for taking the time even to consider this book worth your time. We are hopeful that it might impact your life in some way as it did ours. We want to address a few things first that we hope will make reading this book more enjoyable and beneficial.

Even though we have left out much concerning the specifics of our individual stories, it won't take you long to realize that the contents came from very personal places and spaces. We have lived what we are writing. And, we are still learning so much more than these pages can capture. Some of the concepts and perspectives you will read may relate to you more than others. That's ok. Depending on what season of life and set of circumstances we found ourselves in, it was true for us as well. Our strategy for what is included and omitted is to provide a greater opportunity for the Holy Spirit to work creatively and masterfully on the canvas of your own heart.

Some might wonder the more specific meaning of a reframe in the context of this book. It's a cause and effect type encounter and experience. Merriam Webster Dictionary defines a reframe like this:

> Reframe- to frame (something) again, and often in a different way.[1]

Linda and Charlie Bloom wrote an article in Psychology Today and defined a reframe in these words: *"When we change our point of view on any given situation, the facts remain*

---

[1] Merriam-Webster Online Dictionary, copyright by Merriam-Webster, Incorporated, www.merriam-webster.com, 2015, https://www.merriam-webster.com/dictionary/reframe.

the same, but a deliberate shift is made in how we see it."[2]

A reframe in this context is seeing the picture the way it is designed to be seen so it can be experienced in its fullest capacity. This picture is life itself. It's about experiencing life here and now, and in the scope of eternity. It's foundational for experiencing freedom and fullness in Christ.

Here is one critical item we want to address. We know some believe that their version or translation of the Bible is the best, maybe even the only accurate one. We want to set your minds at ease about the different translations we use in this book. Some translations claim to be "word-for-word" in their interpretations. That is quite impossible. There are so many words that just cannot be translated from Hebrew to Aramaic, to Greek then to English. Some come closer to capturing the actual translation from its original cultural and historical context. However, they may miss out on practical understanding and application today in our cultural and historical context. That's where other translations may be more helpful. Andy Naseli in his book *"How To Understand and Apply The New Testament"* says (paraphrasing), that all translations can be critiqued because none of them are perfect. At best, Bible translations are extremely complicated.

We agree. Some translations communicate better concepts and truths with specific passages than others. And, this is precisely what we are using them for in this book. We are not advocating for one over another, and are certainly not claiming this book as an in-depth Bible study. Time and history have proved that the Holy Spirit is powerful enough to make the Word of God transform lives, no matter the translation. :-)

We hope you enjoy the Word of God in all the different ways God has given man the ability to read, write, understand and speak it. And, we pray this book supports and sheds light on the powerful truths He has given you in His Word.

---

2   Bloom, Linda, L.C.S.W., and Bloom, Charlie, M.S.W., "Reframing - The transformative power of suffering," www.psychologytoday.com, December 14, 2017, retrieved February 3, 2018, https://www.psychologytoday.com/us/blog/stronger-the-broken-places/201712/reframing.

CONTENTS

Acknowledgements v
Preface.. ix
Introduction xvii

SECTION 1
 Establishing The Reframe

　CHAPTER 1
　Foundations 1

　CHAPTER 2
　Fruit..13

　CHAPTER 3
　Wanting...19

　CHAPTER 4
　Realignment Required.......................................25

SECTION 2
 Making The Major Reframes

　CHAPTER 5
　The Bible..37

　CHAPTER 6
　The Triune God..53

　CHAPTER 7
　It's Personal...71

　CHAPTER 8
　Prayer...91

SECTION 3
The Church Reframed

CHAPTER 9
The Church - Part 1 101

CHAPTER 10
The Church - Part 2 113

CHAPTER 11
The Church - Part 3 121

CHAPTER 12
The Church - Part 4 137

SECTION 4
Living The Reframed Life

CHAPTER 13
Celebrate The Seasons 159

CHAPTER 14
All In 171

CHAPTER 15
Secret To Success 181

CHAPTER 16
New, Next Or Nothing 191

Appendix...201
7 Major Milestones..203
About the Authors 211

INTRODUCTION

What if what you are seeing isn't all there is? Does the idea of seeing and experiencing more in this life excite you? Scare you? The truth is we are all guilty of framing life through the foggy lens of this earth. We frame every mountain we conquer and every valley we crawl out of according to the sum total of the thoughts, emotions, and experiences we have in each moment. We frame individual experiences as good or bad, success or failure, and all according to whatever standard we are currently buying into at the time. We will carefully fit each experience into a neatly crafted, perfectly placed frame, and either put it on display for all to celebrate or hide it deep in the recesses of things forgotten in those dark and hidden spaces.

However, what if life is more than what we see through our smudged lenses? What if we are genuinely seeing our life's events dimly, as Paul (the apostle) says in 1 Corinthians 13? What if, indeed, we only know the truth of our experiences in part? What if our poor vision creates frames that are crooked at best and need the right adjustment from The God Who Sees? What if we need to submit our every thought, action, and circumstance to the only One who is Truth Himself?

As the fundamental structure of the wild wild west church continues to unravel, people are finding more and more reasons to leave the organized church (often calling it organized religion). We are one voice among many who believe God is calling us back to His Word, His ways, and His will. This will always be part of the effectiveness of a healthy Gospel-centric person, family, and church in any culture or context.

Reframe allows you to enter a narrative of restoration—one filled with freedom, hope, purpose, fulfillment, peace, and joy! True belief always results in action. Always! This book aims to be a clear voice- an instrument for fine-tuning. A steady and light weapon for fighting the enemy. A source of encouragement and hope through the acts of God's gracious and powerful work.

A healthy reframe has both relational and theological components. Theology comes out of a relational construct/context. Otherwise, it is a perspective that is based on limited knowledge alone. Part of a reframe is to be careful not to focus only on one section within the frame. This can lead to creating your own picture. Also, a reframe is like refocusing a lens. The more we mature, the more we can focus on the complete picture in its entirety. This mindset protects us from allowing anything else into that frame or picture.

Here's the deal, we believe there is an uprising of people today who are no longer satisfied living within the lines that were not created by God. Frames and narratives are created all the time to suit the perspectives and preferences of man. However, they will always leave you short of all that God has intended for you! You have been created for so much more! And, when you encounter the Lord in a new and fresh way, and when you allow the Holy Spirit to reframe your worldview, you will then experience the fullness of life in the way your heart was created for.

Life Out Of The Box

Learning more about God's design for quality of life in the "here and now" is part of a healthy reframe. This is a significant catalyst for people being set free to live life more abundantly. Are you striving for quality in this life and missing it or never attaining it? If so, you may be living in a box. You may be unaware, or even denying the reality of a new paradigm or reframe.

We're all dying, but few are living in the process. A key need for this reframe comes from too many years spent living in a box created by man. Living in a box is exhausting, confusing and just plain foolish. Boxes keep you too pragmatic, unnecessarily structured, packaged, etc. Life in the box seems to work ok until there is a tragedy or significant life-challenging event. Then hard choices have to be made. Where does the incredible work of the Holy Spirit come in here? You see, living in a box seems to leave so little room for the essential and fulfilling work of Christ to be experienced and lived out.

Life out of the box is all about making the most of every opportunity (Ephesians 5:15-16). The psalmist in Psalm 90:12 (noted as a prayer of Moses) expresses a desire to reframe his concept of time on earth. As a result, he would have a heart of wisdom (verse 12). We can see examples of people living with a real "quality of life" mentality throughout the Psalms. This perspective expresses our heart throughout this book. It's one more step towards walking in the ways and wisdom of God!

Psalm 146:2 reveals this irresistible desire to praise God and sing high praises to Him every day. Wow! Praising God all your days, walking in obedience to His Word and living out of His prosperity and success- now that's a reframe worth making! That is a real and worthwhile life lived outside the box.

GETTING STARTED

We pray that this book helps bridge the gap between where you are and where God wants you to be. And, how you start a journey or endeavor has everything to do with the success of it. We have started many things in our lives that were off ever-so-slightly. It doesn't take being off by much for it all to come undone down the road. We see this so clearly in the life of Solomon.

Solomon had such a great start (although he did not end that way). As imperfect as he was from the beginning, God saw something in Solomon that was worthy of emulation. Let's take a quick look at this incredible story.

After David crowns Solomon as King, David dies. Solomon knew that he had some big shoes to fill. There was plenty Solomon didn't know. However, when God confronts him in a dream and says, "Ask what I shall give you," Solomon knew what to ask. He could have asked for anything. Maybe a bigger, stronger army? Perhaps he should have asked for a bigger kingdom to rule? Maybe more wives? More toys?

Faster horses? The best of… whatever? Of course, you know what he asked of God.

> *1 Kings 3:9 (ESV) Give Your servant therefore an understanding mind to govern Your people, that I may discern between good and evil, for who is able to govern this Your great people?*

He asked for Wisdom! What a good start for Solomon's new assignment. But wait! There's more (No, this is not an infomercial for a free knife if you order now). God didn't just give him what Solomon asked for. He gave Solomon so much more (1 Kings 4:20-34).

> *1 Kings 4:29 (ESV) And God gave Solomon wisdom and understanding beyond measure, and breadth of mind like the sand on the seashore.*

So how do you get started? This process of transformation we're calling a reframe requires wisdom and discernment that can only come from God. The Holy Spirit longs to bring this to you. The question is, "are you are willing?" Solomon asked for the very things that opened up even more of God's abundant blessings and gifts. It was the wisdom and discernment God gave that allowed Solomon to have the encounter and experiences he did with God.

Pray and ask the Holy Spirit to make the words on the following pages make sense to you. Ask Him to reveal to you the Father's heart for you. Ask Him to make real to you the promise and reality of Christ in you, and you in Him. You'll need that wisdom and discernment. Otherwise, this will be another book to skim through and forget.

SECTION 1

ESTABLISHING THE REFRAME

CHAPTER 1

FOUNDATIONS

ESTABLISHING THE FRAMEWORK

Reframe was born from a sudden refusal to believe that our lives were nothing more than the chaotic result of the actions caused by those standing against us. Rather, our reframe revealed a purposeful journey that was directed by our Father who was actively working all things for our good and His glory. God had to reframe the lie that everything was happening "to" us by revealing the truth that all things were happening "for" us. Every pain has purpose and every hurt holds healing. Jesus reveals more of Himself through each trial, and He lovingly forges us through the fire in order to make us more like Him.

Be honest, do you get tired of your own narrative? Do you ever find yourself looking back and giving credit to others for your circumstances rather than honoring God as the One ordering your steps and directing your path? Are you sick of giving mere mortals that much power over the trajectory of your life? You must choose to believe that you are either held in the hands of a Sovereign and Almighty God, or you are not. You have to take God at His Word that He is for you and that He has good works for you, created in Christ Jesus before you took your first breath (Ephesians 2:10). Maybe it's time to make the choice to heed the warning we see in Isaiah.

> *Isaiah 2:22 (ESV) Stop regarding man who has breath in his nostrils, of what account is he?*

Why do we give mankind so much credit? Why are we so fearful waiting for the next bad thing to come our way? Why do we walk around with a defeated internal narrative? Do we serve the resurrected King, or not? Do we have the same power that conquered the grave living in us, or not? Until we rightly reframe the events of our past, we will never be able to walk in the fullness of Christ in the present. And, it will only hold us captive from stepping into the good works prepared for us in our future. We need a taste of freedom. We need to believe, receive and live in the reality Paul tells the church in Galatia.

> *Galatians 5:1 (TPT) Let me be clear, the Anointed One has set us free—not partially, but completely and wonderfully free! We must always cherish this truth and stubbornly refuse to go back into the bondage of our past.*

The freeing work of Christ has already been accomplished on the cross. The responsibility to stand firm and receive this gift in its fullness is our choice. Will we remain a victim— a slave to worry, anxiety, dread, confusion and the likes? Or, will we walk confidently as a victor— embracing each and every season God has so faithfully brought us through? And, will we realize that every last moment is for our good and for His glory? What if we chose to make a conscious effort to change our inner narrative and start taking God at His word? We'll find out really quick that He is faithful (2 Timothy 2:13). He is trustworthy (Proverbs 3:5-6). He is a good Father (1 John 3:1). He will never leave us nor forsake us (Hebrews 13:5b).

Know this; our difficult seasons can serve as an act of

God's grace FOR us. The purpose of struggle is ultimately for our liberation. God's first and foremost desire for us is our freedom. Only free people will seek to free people. Strangely enough, God's children seem to be ever-willing to move away from that which is painful. Sometimes the hand of God comes in affliction so the Holy Spirit can correct our course and get us back to walking in His ways. We must choose to surrender to this course correction if we are ever going to walk in the fullness of Christ.

> *Psalm 119:71 (ESV) It was good for me that I was afflicted, that I might learn your statutes.*

Here's a fun fact for you. Once we reframe our past, we are then free to release past offenses. We realize people are just people. We are merely broken, imperfect children of dust. Fortunately, our perfect, loving, pure and Holy God directs our paths. We no longer need to point fingers and blame others for our circumstances. We stop regarding man, and we start remembering God. We begin to walk in the joy of Jesus, knowing we are fully known and loved by the Creator who formed our inner parts and knitted us together in our mother's womb (Psalm 139:13-24). He is El Roi (Hebrew); the God Who Sees. This means not one single event of your life escapes His watchful eye.

Friends, know this; God brings us only that which is necessary to free us from oppressive structures (our own or external), so we can then speak freedom to others and offer them the same hope. That is our purpose, and that is His plan— the free setting other captives free (Isaiah 61).

Reframe. What's it about? It's about learning to change your inner narrative. Let's dive in and establish some framework for your new reframe.

REBUILD FROM THE FOUNDATION UP!

The foundation is essential to the functionality of any structure (faith or belief system). If you have excellent materials, exceptional workmanship, but a weak foundation, your structure fails. Let's take a spiritual inventory and see what's built within the walls of your faith. What truths are you holding on to? What is currently motivating you, pushing you forward, and spurring you on as you face each day?

As we walk with Christ, we have all kinds of external influences that contribute to our belief system. We have our pastors or spiritual gurus of choice. We have books and articles without end. And don't forget, we have the infinite wisdom of the internet continually streaming into our lives. So what are you holding fast to in this current season of life?

Wherever you find yourself on your faith walk today, you have to go back down the proverbial "stairs" to your foundation to better understand how you've ended up on the current ground you've chosen. Wherever you are regarding the maturity of your relationship with Jesus, know this— you don't have to stay there. Where we plant our feet is ultimately our choice. That is why it's so vital to check the foundation that we've allowed ourselves to build our lives on. Let's take a look at what God says about the importance of the right foundation.

SAND OR STONE?

There is a great parable told by Jesus in the Bible. There are several different translations that do it justice, but there is something simple and powerful in the way it's communicated in The Message:

> *Matthew 7:24-27 (MSG) 24-25 These words I speak to you are not incidental additions to your life, homeowner improvements to your standard of living. They are foundational words, words to build a life on. If you work these words into your life, you are like a smart carpenter who built his house on solid rock. Rain poured down, the river flooded, a tornado hit—but nothing moved that house. It was fixed to the rock. 26-27 "But if you just use my words in Bible studies and don't work them into your life, you are like a stupid carpenter who built his house on the sandy beach. When a storm rolled in and the waves came up, it collapsed like a house of cards."*

This parable is not just about the sand, the rock, and the house. It's pretty simple. It's about making two choices.

- Are you wise or foolish? (This determines what you do with the next set of choices.)
- Are you obedient or disobedient?

Why is the foundation so important? The foundation is what determines whether or not the structure it's built on can hold up against all the elements of life. In this case, the wind and the rain (even tornados).

The Rock= Truth (Jesus Himself)

The Sand= Man's best efforts (religious or otherwise)

Jesus presents another powerful set of choices and their consequences earlier in this chapter.

Matthew 7:13-14 (TPT) 13 Come to God through the narrow gate, because the wide gate and broad path is the way that leads to destruction—nearly everyone chooses that crowded road! 14 The narrow gate and the difficult way leads to eternal life—so few even find it!

Principle 1: You will live life as a wise person, or as a foolish one.

The word "wise" comes from the Greek word "phronimos"; having the capacity to understand, often in the daily things of life; wise in spiritual matters. The word for "foolish" comes from the Greek word "moros"; lacking in sense, judgement or discretion; foolish or stupid.

Principle 2: You will either hear and obey, or hear and carry on with life as you see fit.

To hear is more than just being aware audibly that someone has spoken. Jesus is using the word "akouein"; to gain knowledge of by hearing; to take testimony from. So, once the truth has been spoken, once you are exposed to the things of God, you have "heard." Now you are responsible for that knowledge.

Being wise or foolish is predicated on whether or not you hear and respond with obedience or disobedience. How can we know if we are building our lives/house on the Rock (Jesus), or the sand (self)? Wouldn't you want to know before the end of your life if you were building a house of cards?

Okay, there aren't many people who would confess to being foolish or stupid. Choosing to live life according to self isn't something many Christians would confess as their life's story. However, the pages being written in it may say otherwise. So, the underlying assumption is that you are building upon your life. This has inseparable ties with Matthew 6:19-21 (treasures in Heaven) and Galatians 6:6-10 (reaping what we sow).

These are the essential beliefs of storing up treasure in Heaven which is permanent and reaping accordingly to how and what you sow. You can't live life according to your plans and desires then expect God to make them prosper.

For the sake of space and time, simply put, living life as a wise person is staying connected in fellowship with Jesus (John 15:5), which we'll address more in a later chapter. It is only from within this connection that you can hear and sense the heart of God. The fruit from this relationship includes peace, direction, hope, freedom, purpose, and the ability to live life to the full. The Spirit of God helps us know Him, love Him, and follow Him. All our decisions are made from here—if indeed we are wise by hearing and obeying. Your house is being built on the Rock.

However, living life as a foolish person is nothing more than living life outside the context of a spirit-filled love relationship with Jesus. It's simply a matter of listening to everything and everyone and then making your own decisions apart from the leadership of the Holy Spirit and the Word of God. The good news? You have already been warned throughout the Bible concerning the results of this choice. The results include separation, loneliness, lack of power and peace, a false sense of purpose and success, destruction, and death.

O, and the storms? Yes, they will come. Whether you are a wise or foolish builder, they will come. Nobody is exempt from the tornados of this life. It seems that some get hit more than others, but they're inevitable. They all have the potential to destroy and tear apart anything and anyone. James gives us great advise on the attitude and outlook we should have when they come (James 1:2-8). He tells us that these difficulties are invaluable opportunities that result in great joy. In that same passage, he tells us that our faith being tested results in power being stirred up in us that provides endurance, strength, maturity, wisdom, and confidence (in our faith).

God's pure, perfect, and unfailing Word must be our chosen foundation on which we frame the rest of our existence— our faith, our values, our operating system. These verses right here hold great promise for us as Christ-followers. If we absorb God's Word into our very DNA, taking it in daily and living it out as we go about our day, we are building our lives on an unshakable foundation.

Unshakable? That Word might mean something more to you if your land is plagued with fault lines, as ours is here in California. We've seen and felt first hand what a sudden, unexpected shake can do to a structure, a family, or even an entire city. Are you finding yourself in a season of shaking? Has there been a sudden unexpected jolt to your "norm?" Our ability to thrive in chaos will directly correlate to what we've set our hope on. Is it Jesus? Just Jesus? Just the overwhelming, never-ending, reckless love of Jesus? Are we fully trusting him to hold up the structure of our lives? Have we anchored our framework into the solid Rock of Ages so that we are better equipped to stand firm when, and not if, the storm comes?

This passage also holds a different promise for those choosing to establish their framework on a different foundation. Which foundation, you ask? Anything other than Jesus. The world. Friends. Family. Careers. Social status. Social media. The result of trusting in anything other than the unchangeable God and His perfect Word is always the same-collapse.

Isn't that a great image? Collapse. Total devastation. A structure was taken down to its starting place. It makes us think of ancient Roman ruins, with nothing left but broken columns not fit to hold the weight of a bird, much less a wall. Collapse. All you hoped for, all the endless hours of striving, all the blood, sweat and tears, all of it for nothing. But aren't we already promised that outcome in John 15:5? Jesus could not possibly tell us any more plainly: "Apart from me you can do nothing." When we choose to ignore His Word, sidestep His commands and go our own way, we are somehow still shocked and dismayed to watch our efforts come to ruin. Why are we surprised? Our good Father has shown us openly in His Word our only hope of standing firm in the chaos of life. It is found in the foundation of knowing and loving Him, and absorbing and living out His Word.

So the question is simple; In each waking moment, are you exercising the mental discipline (or self-control, as seen in Galatians 5) by responding to the Holy Spirit? Do you measure all your daily circumstances up against the Truth found in His Word? Maybe the ultimate question is- are you believing Jesus, and taking Him at His Word. You see, you can fill your head with knowledge of chapters and verses all day long, but until you internalize each letter as a love letter written directly to you from your Creator, you will not be experiencing the fullness of God's Word coming to life within you.

You cannot experience the springs of Living Water from the Spirit flowing in and through you until you believe and receive the Truth for yourself down to the very core of your being. Your ever-growing relationship with the God of the universe must be the immovable, unshakable foundation that you firmly plant your feet upon every day. This is a non-negotiable if you are to go any further in experiencing this reframe.

FROM FOUNDATIONS TO FULLNESS

Paul had the daunting task of shepherding a flock of spiritual infants. The organized New Testament churches were budding across the region with new gatherings popping up in homes each day, producing thousands of new Christ-followers in an extraordinarily brief amount of time. One could assume that the question on everyone's lips echoed the same: "What now, Paul? What is our purpose? What does Jesus want us to do now?" We see that Paul had but one prayer for his fledgling flock: to know the fullness of God.

Ephesians 3:14-21 gives us such a clear picture of Paul's deep desire for those to whom he was writing. His prayer for them was the God would grant them strength through the power of the Holy Spirit so that Christ would be released deep within them. They would then be empowered to experience the enduring and far-reaching love of Jesus. As a result, the fullness of God would consume them and they could experience far more than they could ever have imagined.

The expanded point and purpose of needing a reframe is:

FREEDOM & FULLNESS IN CHRIST!

Paul desperately wanted more than small tribes of religious clones with empty hearts and full heads. He wanted the very life of Christ to dwell in their hearts through faith so that they would be rooted and grounded in His love. Here we are, back to the right foundation again! Paul wanted their roots to grow deep down into the fertile soil of God's great love. This would give them the spiritual health and strength to comprehend the greatness of God's immeasurable gift of grace, and to help them truly know the expansive love of Christ personally— each one taking full ownership of the love of God poured out upon them.

What happens when we root ourselves in the Truth of God's eternal, mysterious love We are prepared and ready to be filled with the fullness of God! There is a deep, rich fullness that awaits those who choose to dive deeper into God's Word, knowing His unchangeable Truth on a heart level, and not just as words on a page. There is a fullness that comes with the Spirit revealing the matchless love of God. It's this fullness that will allow us to walk in pure freedom, knowing the Creator of the universe completely and wholeheartedly loves us for all eternity. He is our covenant-keeping God whose promise to love us and build a heavenly place for us can never be broken— not by any of our thoughts, words or deeds. He keeps His promises at all times for His own name's sake.

By His Spirit, we are alive and free. Free indeed is what Galatians 5:1 says we are. For freedom, Christ has set us free. And in John 8:36 we are told that if the Son has set us free, then we are free indeed.

It is so important that we experience the fullness of Christ, which then releases us to walk in our freedom in Christ. Did you get that? Read that statement again. See, if we are free, we will speak of this freedom to others. If we are bound, we will attempt to bind others with the same chains we wear. With every encounter, we bind people to us with cords of our every expectation, or we release them into freedom to walk with the Spirit and let Him guide His children as He sees fit. Will we speak strength, encouragement, and comfort into people, or will we lay heavy yokes of our preference and expectations upon their shoulders?

People's actions and their reactions are not to be what we focus on, as we hear Jesus say here:

> John 21:22 (TPT) Jesus replied, "If I decide to let him live until I return, what concern is that of yours? You must still keep on following Me!"

Every child of God is under the hand and direction of Jesus just like we are. Why do we expect them to look like us, act like us or think like us? They are free indeed and under God's hand. So when we see something we wouldn't do, what is that to us? Why create offense? Why take it personally? Freedom from offense is ours when we are walking in the freedom and fullness of Christ!

The best way to keep from tripping over the block of offense is to stop regarding man altogether! Stop regarding man and start remembering God. It's our enemy that encourages us to live discontent lives, always looking sideways, continually regarding man and comparing. He distracts us with each other, so we forget our individually crafted works that God has prepared beforehand and start judging other people's work. And what is that to us? Why would we even be concerned with anyone else's works? It creates envy, comparison, and discontentment. The tragedy of it is this— it renders us less useful for the work we were created to do in Christ Jesus, and far less fulfilled.

Moving in maturity means growing in our firm foundation to experiencing freedom and fullness in Christ. This is so vital to our spiritual health, and for the health of those around us!

We can only impart to others what's first been given to us. This is why Paul prayed so earnestly that his young believers would seek to know the breadth, height, length, and depth of the rich and glorious love of Christ When we let this truth sink into our marrow, we now have something beautiful and eternal to impart to those around us. But we must first encounter this life-changing truth and love ourselves! And, don't forget what Paul says in Romans 8:37-39. He tells us that we are more than conquerors, and nothing can separate us from the love of God in Christ Jesus.

Today, you are no longer building a house of cards. You are a wise builder, hearing Him and responding in obedience. You are not alone. You are not forsaken (Joshua 1:5). Press on with this confidence, assurance, and encouragement today.

WHAT DO YOU THINK?

What have you believed that established the foundation for what you think and how you live? Is the structural integrity worthy of building your life on?

Are you fulfilled? I mean the kind of fulfillment that God promises us in Christ by the powerful work of the Holy Spirit. Are are you fulfilled? If not, what life materials do you need to change out to establish both a firm foundation and a sturdy, stable satisfying life in Christ?

Are you ready for life more abundantly? Are you ready to stop feeling like everything good keeps getting stolen from you or wrecked beyond repair? A proper reframe regarding your life starts with choosing The Good Shepherd as your foundation.

Check out John 10:1-21 for your ticket to freedom and the beginning of a life more abundant. Now that's a reframe worth making.

CHAPTER 2

FRUIT

DOES IT REALLY MATTER?

Does it really matter? This is the question we ask every day (whether we acknowledge we're doing it or not). Does making a choice to choose how to live my life matter? As we discussed in our last chapter, firm foundations are vital for a strong, sturdy framework and a stable structure.

Two questions noticeably prevalent in Christian life regarding faith and practice: First, does it really matter how I live my life as long as I'm happy? Second, why aren't I experiencing the life I read about in the Bible or hear at church?

Let's start with the obvious— fruit is a product of something. It is the summation or result of the current condition of the tree or plant. Another critical fact to consider is the source and sustenance that tree is drawing from. The fruit can't lie. It always tells the truth of the current state of health and gives evidence to all that has been happening to it. This paradigm is understood clearly in Luke 6:43-46.

THE REALITY (LUKE 6:43)

"You will never" are some pretty weighty words. Jesus tells us in His own words a cold hard fact; "You'll never find choice fruit hanging on a bad, unhealthy tree." Therefore, the fruit of our lives externally reflects our condition internally. At the same time, this is a forward-looking statement because just like some trees have bad years and produce a weak harvest, that same tree can also turn around and have a big year and produce a healthy harvest. It's not doomed to one condition or the other. It's merely a reflection of its current state of health. This is why our fruit matters— it is a self-awareness check.

Establishing the laws at hand as factual, nonfictional, and not subject to interpretation is critical to the life and health of any person (or tree in this example). It seems like every generation since the beginning of time believes they will be the ones to be the exception and break God's universal laws. Let's talk briefly about an example almost all of us can relate to.

Kids of all ages believe they are "different." They think they have figured out a way to cross the lines and expect not to experience repercussion. They believe they can taste the evil and not long for it. They think they can play with fire and not at some point get burned. You get the picture. Sadly, this follows us even into adulthood. It just looks more grown up and sophisticated (well, sometimes). That also makes it easier for us to justify our rebellious actions. I can cheat on my taxes, and since it's not hurting anyone, it's okay. I can have that borderline inappropriate relationship with a co-worker, and it won't be a big deal. Friends, it's a big deal. It will become an even bigger deal when the fruit shows itself. Every action produces fruit. Let us say that again. EVERY ACTION PRODUCES FRUIT! What is done in secret will eventually be made known. Deeds done in darkness will one day find themselves exposed in the light. How have we not learned this in the thousands of years we've been around?

So here's another goal of the reframed life— "Choice Fruit!" The action point of our lives is to be ambassadors of Christ. It's not for ourselves. It's not for our glory. All fruit is for His glory. It should be our heart's desire to live a life that reflects the heart of God, truth of Christ, and the power of the

Holy Spirit. 2 Peter 3:11 tells us that we are to be consumed with holiness, and how vital it is to live a holy life. We can't emphasize enough how crucial it is to live as though a great revelation is coming. Why? Because Jesus has already proclaimed in these next verses, a reckoning is on its' way.

THE REVELATION (LUKE 6:44-45)

Toby Slough (Pastor of Cross Timbers Church in Argyle, TX) once shared this gem in a service we attended, "You can't plant tomatoes and pray for corn." And, he's also the guy that said: "You can't eat a Cheeto and pray for God to transform it into a carrot."[3] Love that guy. Well, Jesus says it like this:

> Luke 6:44-45 (NLT) 44 A tree is identified by its fruit. Figs are never gathered from thornbushes, and grapes are not picked from bramble bushes. 45 A good person produces good things from the treasury of a good heart, and an evil person produces evil things from the treasury of an evil heart. What you say flows from what is in your heart.

Just as the fruit falling from a tree reveals its true nature, your true nature will too be exposed by what falls from your branches. Here's a question; what's falling from your branches? Galatians 5:16-23 is a great litmus test. Paul tells the Galatians in that passage that if we walk by the Spirit, we will not gratify the desires of our flesh. This is true because of the simple fact that the desires of the flesh and the Spirit are diametrically opposed. He goes on in that passage to give examples of someone walking according to the Spirit or the flesh.

Just as people gather fruit in the harvest season, what are people gathering from you in this season? Is it helpful? Harmful? Is your family better because of it? Is it building up the body of Christ? Or, are you a stumbling block and causing illness and ineffectiveness? Regardless, your condition is being made known. That's why this word "revealed" is such

3   Slough, Toby, Pastor at Cross Timbers Community Church, Argyle, TX, Sermon from 2103.

a powerful promise.

Your choices determine your fruitfulness and your effectiveness. The option is not in whether or not you will bear good or bad fruit. This is only the product or results of your choices in how you have invested in your heart. Jesus says there are only two options.

OPTION 1 - TRUTH (God's Word to you) STORED IN YOUR HEART...

Psalm 119:11 (ESV) I have stored up your Word in my heart that I might not sin against you.

Our only weapon in a fallen world is to stand on God's Truth. It's our only protection from false religion, traditions of men, trappings of false doctrine, etc. It's also life-giving. This Word is alive and active. Notice what the Bible says.

Hebrews 4:12-13 (TPT) For we have the living Word of God, which is full of energy, and it pierces more sharply than a two-edged sword. It will even penetrate to the very core of our being where soul and spirit, bone and marrow meet! It interprets and reveals the true thoughts and secret motives of our hearts. There is not one person who can hide their thoughts from God, for nothing that we do remains a secret, and nothing created is concealed, but everything is exposed and defenseless before his eyes, to whom we must render an account.

This is a willful response to a work initiated by the Holy Spirit. This is not started or activated by the human will. It's only when we submit our will to the guidance of the Holy Spirit that will we be open to the Word of God.

OPTION 2 - LIES (Satan's Narrative for you) HIDDEN IN THEIR HEARTS...

Genesis 3:10 (ESV) And he said, I heard the sound of you in the garden, and I was afraid, because I was naked, and I hid myself.

Hiding is not new. Satan was right there from the beginning ready to create a narrative for humanity different from God's. The narrative was to believe there was more available than what God was offering. In other words, God was hiding things from them, and they could have access to it by disobeying Him. In a strange twist of fate, believing that lie caused them to hide from God. So we see that our hiding will reveal the byproduct of the fruit of sin. Who do we think we're fooling?

THE RESPONSE (LUKE 6:46)

This verse is short and sweet. Jesus asks a direct question: "Why do you repeatedly call me Lord when you don't do what I say?" The only right and correct response to any master is complete obedience. How much more so should this be our posture and position as followers of Christ? Storing up God's Word does not mean storing it away in a storage unit to be left unused and neglected. Rather, submitting to God's Word and storing it up in our hearts will lead to action, specifically obedience to what Jesus has already taught us. Question: what good is God's truth to an individual if they don't hear it?

There is also this misconception we believe down deep, but would probably not say out loud— we believe that we can live in a way contrary to what the Bible teaches and not be found out. The apostle Paul had to remind the church in Galatia that God could not be mocked. The truth is, whatever they planted, they would harvest. If it was good seed they planted, it would be good fruit they would have at harvest time. But, the opposite is true as well (Galatians 6:7-8).

DOES IT REALLY MATTER?

Look again at the questions from the beginning of this chapter:

Does it really matter how I live my life as long as I'm happy?

Why aren't I experiencing the life I read about in the Bible or hear at church?

What does the fruit in your life say about you right now? Want that to change at all? If you and I are going to experience and live this fruitful life, then what we are storing up in our hearts, minds, and bodies really does matter.

Maybe a Reframe for you could include the following:

Being intentional in what you're storing up.

Making choices that graciously afford you the fruit of the Spirit (Galatians 5:22-23) and the fruit of righteousness (Philippians 1, Hebrews 12:11, James 3:18, Proverbs 11:30, Amos 6:12).

Remembering that as individuals we must choose each day who we will fear and serve with all sincerity and faithfulness (Joshua 24:14-15).

CHAPTER 3

WANTING

WHAT DO YOU REALLY WANT?

Have you ever wondered why it is that when you have what you want, you find yourself still wanting? When what you want is what you already have, shouldn't you not be in want? Here's a good question: Is your life driven by what you have or what you want? Both of these can become obsessive.

What do you really want? Ok, so now are you willing to do what it takes to get it? We would love to tell you that we have always wanted the right things and have been consistent in doing what it takes to get it. But, we cannot. When you are not walking in the freedom for which Jesus set you free, you can't experience the fullness of what it means to be wholly abandoned to Him, and Him alone. These are things that many people think they understood, but find out later in their spiritual journey they knew very little about. And, now that we know how important investing in our lives as followers of Christ is, we can see the fruit from that by what we want, and what we are willing to do (or not do) to experience it.

Make no mistake; we will all ultimately do what we want to do. This sounds like a crazy concept, but follow along. Every choice we make is a direct reflection of what we want at that moment, regardless of what we say we want. Adam and Eve made a choice based on what they wanted at that moment. So many of the Old Testament Judges and Kings expressed their desire to follow after God but didn't tear down the altars and sacrificial systems to other gods. So they said they wanted to follow God, but not really. Not completely anyway. See how "want" is so complex and often convoluted? We can say in one breath that we want to abandon all for the sake of Christ. We can say we want to be all in. But then we look at our lives and often look like the people described in Matthew 23:27-28. Jesus calls out the religious leaders and tells them they are hypocrites. Why? Because they looked great on the outside but were filled with impurities and lawlessness on the inside.

Make no mistake, what we want changes our trajectory and guides our feet. Look at what Jesus said to His disciples when they too expressed their wanting to follow Him.

> *Luke 9:23 (TPT) Jesus said to all of His followers, "If you truly desire to be My disciple, you must disown your life completely, embrace My 'cross' as your own, and surrender to My ways."*

Did you see that? Jesus said they had first to disown their life entirely. Next, He said they had to embrace His cross as their own. Lastly, He told them to surrender to His ways (implying following Him).

Our flesh is going to want to reframe this to suit what makes us happy by earthly and fleshly standards. We will attempt to take ownership of our own lives but still expect His provisions. We'll want to forgo anything uncomfortable and painful, and yet, expect the growth and maturity that would come from it. And, we want to be in control of the plans and purposes for our lives, but still, expect the benefits of His ways. Again, these are things we would not say out loud. However, for too many of us, this has been the actual fruit falling from our branches.

So, What Do You Really Want? Alan Hirsch in his book "5Q" says;

> "If you want transformational Gospel movement—really want it—then you are going to have to unlearn some very ancient churchly habits and be willing to relearn some new—and yet paradoxically more ancient—more authentically biblical ones."[4]

What if you could trade what you have for what you really want? Then, if it's really, really what you want, you'd be fulfilled. Right? Philippians 3:1-11 provides excellent insight into the world of want. Paul tells the church in Philippi that there are those in the world who operate in the flesh causing great harm to others. He then tells followers of Christ they are to put no confidence in the flesh. Let's break it down a little more. Here are two perspectives Paul gives us in this passage: What I have and what I want.

What I Have

We are free - therefore we should be the people rejoicing the most. But there's a force/movement against those of us who want to live and rejoice in that freedom. In Paul's day and time, they were called the Judaizers (dogs, evil, mutilators of the flesh). You can even want something good and right, go about it incorrectly, and never fully receive it. This is Paul's warning to us. It's not "Jesus and whatever else" for salvation, love, and life. It's always been and will forever be Jesus ONLY.

It's not because of us. Paul placed no confidence in his flesh (even though his credentials were second to none). Paul had it all— purpose, position, popularity, power, possessions. What happened next is amazing. He encounters Jesus through a blinding light which changed his world forever. What he wanted from that day forward was opposed to his former life of want.

---

4   Hirsch, Alan, 5Q: Reactivating the Original Intelligence and Capacity of the Body of Christ, location 448 of 5907 Kindle, 100M, 2017.

WHAT I WANT

In Philippians 3:7-11, Paul cuts his losses. Meaning, he cut his tie to any foundation other than Jesus. If what you want is anything other than Jesus, your wanting will result in rubbish. What value system can you place on this world that can compare to the surpassing worth of knowing Jesus Christ your Lord?

Everyone is willing to put forth effort towards what they really want. So what do you want? The apostle Paul said that he just wanted to know Christ. This was no casual knowledge he was after. He said he wanted to know Christ in His suffering, even to the point of death. However, Paul also knew that he would know Christ in His power and resurrection (Philippians 3:10-11)!

When what you want is to obey and please God (in your marriage, your parenting, your relationships, your job, etc.), you will experience fullness and victory. What you want is what you'll end up doing— what you really want that is. It's what you place the most value on. That's what you want. And, that's what you'll work towards. John tell us in the third chapter; "He must increase, but I must decrease."

So what do you do when your wantor is off? Let's look at this in two parts:

PART 1: WHAT'S THE PROBLEM?

James 4:1-5 answers this with great conviction. We're told that ultimately it's our desires and jealousy that rages within us that causes conflicts and quarrels. In other words, we want what we want and are willing to scheme and harm others to get it. Sometimes we even go to God and express what we want, but don't receive it in return because of our motives. We often want selfishly.

This is where so much conflict within relationships is born! And it seems to me that most the time people that are still in wanting cannot clearly articulate what it is they really want. So they keep wanting. Do you want half-heartedly? Do you want it? What's keeping you from being free to want Jesus only? What's going on in your minds that are obstacles and hurdles?

PART 2: WHAT'S THE SOLUTION?

James gives us this as well in James 4:6-10. He starts off by summarizing what the problem is again- PRIDE! And we know that God resists the proud. So the answer is obvious— HUMILITY! When we submit to God out of a heart of humility, He provides a grace that allows us to stand up against the enemy. The fruit from this transformation is maturity and greater intimacy with and dependency on our Heavenly Father.

Friends, what do you really want? What do you want as the people of God, the church? There is only one way to really get what you really want. James gives us the steps to this:

- Submit to God.
- Resist the devil.
- Draw near to God.
- Confess and Repent.
- Humble yourselves (before the Lord).

All of this can be summed up in one word— SURRENDER. Don't get us wrong, surrender is hard. Isn't it? This will forever change your want or, what you want, and what happens to you when you get what you want. Then, ultimately what you will really want is for Him to save you and redeem you. It will be to know Him and make Him known.

Do you realize what this means? What you really want (the real need) is at the core of what you're trying to say you want (the felt / perceived need). The core need is always a right relationship with Jesus. The core answer to every need is a right relationship in Jesus. Security in Jesus. Identity in Jesus. Faith hope and love in Jesus. Purpose in Jesus. Companionship with Jesus. And, on and on the benefits go. The only way these ongoing needs are met is in Jesus— receiving and giving His unconditional love. He loves you perfectly, wholly, fully, everlastingly, continually, and consistently. Break down the defenses. Remove the doubt, unbelief, and resistance.

SO, WHAT DO YOU WANT?

To answer this question in a way that provides breakthrough and sustainability, consider and take personally what Jesus wants from you and for you:

...to believe Him!

...to receive Him!

...to follow Him!

...to trust Him!

...to love Him!

A significant part of a transformational Reframe is to align yourself to believing He has His best for you. If you do, then it will be much more natural to live by the Spirit because you will want what you have already determined is best— Jesus!

Check out these fantastic passages of Scripture that will assist you in your Reframe for wanting the things of God!

Psalm 27:4 / Psalm 37:1-9 / Hebrews 10:23-25 / 1 John 5:14-16

*What other passages come to mind when you think of wanting the things of God?

CHAPTER 4

REALIGNMENT REQUIRED

LIVING IN THE FULLNESS OF CHRIST!

Realignment: when we realize something is out of line within us that keeps pulling us down a wrong path— whether mental, emotional, spiritual or physical.

When we gain proper perspective, that is a proper reframe; we can move into realigning our lives to the life God wants us to live. Now that's a healthy reframe.

Think of it like rebranding. Companies of all kinds spend an immense amount of money to rebrand to regain the wayward gaze of the public eye. There are things you have to add, subtract, change, reinvent, etc. They may choose brighter colors for their logo, or they may tone it down to something more modern and subdued. Whichever route they want, a realignment is required. This causes the company to rethink their purpose and their plans. They need to rediscover what they value most as a company, and then create new ways to express this message to the world.

Another way you may think of realignment is with your automobile. When you're driving down the road, and your car wants to take you places you are not choosing to steer, you probably need a realignment. A realignment corrects your car or truck to its intended state or position of operation. There are many reasons why an automobile gets out of alignment. It's mostly because of what it has been through. Rough roads. Abuse. Carelessness. Accidents. When these things happen, a realignment is going to be required. You are wise to see this through as it will ensure maximum performance!

There is a cost associated with these realignments. It takes time. You have to acknowledge that something is off. You have to choose to see that it gets corrected. The Bible would refer to this cost as a sacrifice.

If the great question and answer expressed in the Westminster Shorter Catechism is correct (which although not Biblical text, definitely reflects Biblical truth), then most would agree there is a need for a realignment (or an ongoing one). Here is that excerpt: "Man's chief end is to glorify God, and to enjoy Him forever." This realignment serves as a clear voice, instrument for fine-tuning, a natural and light weapon for fighting the enemy as well as being a source of encouragement and hope. If what you really want is to glorify God and to enjoy Him, yet that is currently not your experience, you might just need a realignment. A great friend of mine (as well as one of our board members) once said;

> "This is the essence of the true Christian faith because it is the essence of the Godhead. If we are not personally aligned with it in our body, soul, and spirit, we cannot fully know God. If our church is not aligned with it, the church cannot fully know God. To be the person God wants us to be depends on alignment." -Cortland Reger[5]

---

5   Reger, Cortland, Reger Physical Therapy, Anchorage, AK, dialogue, 2018.

There is the idea that floats around our brains that we can keep operating out of alignment with God and still get maximum results from Him. We want to dispel that deception for you today. If you want what He has for you, you can't keep doing life your way and expect from God what He promises only to those committed to His ways. His promises and provisions are wrapped up in His purpose and plans. If you're honest, sometimes you intentionally or unintentionally attempt to manipulate God into tailoring His plans and purposes around you and your desires. You want His provisions and promises customized to your preferences. There are a lot of people out there that will do that for you. However, God is not one of them.

His standard is clear. His commands are immovable and are without compromise. Our only response to a Holy and Sovereign God is surrender. When you do, it radically changes what you seek, what you desire, and what you ask for. All of a sudden, His desires become your desires. His ways become your ways. His will becomes your will. And this is reason enough for a realignment.

> *Isaiah 55:8-9 (ESV) For my thoughts are not your thoughts, neither are your ways my ways, declares the Lord. For as the heavens are higher than the earth, so are my ways higher than your ways and my thoughts than your thoughts.*

There are great examples of realignment all throughout scripture. Let's take a look at one in the Old Testament, then one from the New Testament.

OLD TESTAMENT EXAMPLE

Let us introduce you to King David's son, Solomon. Watch the realignment unfold here (1 Kings 3-4).

God began to realign Solomon by first presenting him with a choice (1 Kings 3:3-9). This choice would reveal what was really in Solomon's heart (the fruit that falls from the tree). God met Solomon in a dream and told Him to ask for anything. He chose discernment, knowing good from evil to know best how to lead God's people. He then went to Jerusalem and sacrificed at the ark of the covenant. He was now giving praise and honor at the right place. His request and response was part of his realignment.

Isn't it interesting the conversation that he was having with God IN HIS DREAM! Some people need to hear this today; your life is operating in the wrong place and space, so your ability to dream and to interact with the Lord in this way has been snuffed out (maybe fear, ignorance, doubt, etc.).

Solomon asked for the heavenly things that would serve as a catalyst for God to give earthly things as well— A heart that loved people, discernment (understanding mind) to judge rightly, wisdom (knowledge that brings perspective) to lead people.

> DISCERNMENT: the ability to judge well.
>
> WISDOM: the soundness of an action or decision with regard to the application of experience, knowledge, and good judgment.

Good judgment (discernment) leads to sound decision making (wisdom). This allows you to reframe life, and live it according to that healthy reframe. Could it be that part of our problem as Christian is that we have strayed so far from our original alignment that we no longer sense the deep need for discernment and wisdom from God? Remember, Solomon's motivation wasn't to be the most sought after communicator, leader, prophet, priest or king.

Another significant part of this realignment for Solomon was God's response (3:10-15). God was so pleased with his unselfish request that He gave Solomon the highest wisdom and discernment, but also riches and honor. Out of anything in this world to assure Biblical prosperity— it begins with discernment and wisdom— the practical ability to govern. What good is wealth without wisdom to use it? We see that it pleased the Lord that this young king asked for wisdom. Side note: Solomons father sought the Lord when making decisions. We know the legacy he left for young Solomon. Solomon's request pleased the Lord. This too was part of his realignment.

Lastly, there were results of this new reframe for Solomon. Discernment and wisdom both lead to much-needed peace. The realignment in Solomon's life gave way for the Lord to make much of him, which made much of God. The success Solomon experienced went far beyond himself (which was his goal and motivation from the start). He was not looking to his own interests only.

> *Philippians 2:4 (TPT) Abandon every display of selfishness. Possess a greater concern for what matters to others instead of your own interests.*

Your request is driven and determined by the place and space created by your choosing. Hearing His voice amid the voices directly effects your request, your response, and ultimately the result. It's foolish and presumptuous to assume you have rights and access to the will and ways of God while all along continuing to walk and live out of alignment with Him and His Word.

Here are three questions for you:
- What is your REQUEST?
- What is your RESPONSE?
- What are your RESULTS?

Why is all of this such a big deal? It affects all of eternity! It's a matter of life and death for many, and quality of life for everyone. Friends, God has called us into some deep and crazy waters out there. Without correction and realignment, we can not experience a healthy reframe.

If we do not individually and willfully choose this radical realignment, we absolutely cannot as a community or church. Out there, they are waiting for us. They may not know that, but we do! This is why God has given us our mission.

NEW TESTAMENT EXAMPLE

The reframe in John chapter 6 has to do with self-effort versus the power of God, and the effect on our circumstances.

First, in this chapter we see Jesus wanting to feed a weary and hungry crowd of 5000 (even more when you include women and children). Look closer, and you will find Jesus using this situation to test the faith of his closest friends. Jesus asks his disciples to feed the crowd. Everyone in that small circle of twelve knew that what Jesus was asking from them was utterly and undeniably impossible. Feeding a crowd this size would take an unfathomable amount of resources, and this little ragtag group of nomads certainly didn't have what was needed to feed the masses (so they thought). A simple assessment proved they did not have amongst their belongings the provisions or resources to accomplish what Jesus had asked them to do. One disciple threw out a last-minute observation— a child had five loaves and two fish. Surely as soon as the disciple mentioned it, he realized it wouldn't even feed the twelve. But in a moment, their reality was forever changed.

Self-effort had produced five loaves and two fish. Jesus then took what was available, using what He had on hand, and used it for His glory to be revealed. He used the team He had to prepare the people for His upcoming provision. He asked the team to participate by asking the masses to sit down in small groups. People often wonder what caused the crowd to obey the disciple's request. Maybe they expected that they were going to witness the power of God among them. Perhaps this is why the people sat down. They were front row participants in seeing a revelation that would lead to Jesus' exaltation!

A. Preparation: Notice the act of faith by the disciples as well as the crowd. Remember, Jesus didn't even disclose what He was about to do. He ordered the disciples to move among the masses and set them down. The disciple's minds must have been spinning with possibilities. Is Jesus going to cook? Is He going to create a table out of thin air? What will He do? Regardless, they knew Him enough to know He could be trusted and loved Him enough to obey His request.

B. Expectation: If the disciples didn't fully expect Jesus to meet their need and the needs of others, they could have disobeyed or challenged Jesus, refusing to follow the order to sit down and wait. They could have huddled together and devised their own plans to provide for at least their own needs. They were hungry, too! They could have sought for what they needed among the crowd, trying to meet their needs from other people. However, they walked as examples for the crowd as they simply heard His Word and obeyed Him in expectation.

C. <u>Revelation</u>: Jesus, Himself with the meager rations in His own hands, blessed them before the eyes of His friends and the followers. He met every single need and then some. Jesus' abundant love and power were made manifest "to those who were seated." Those who chose to listen and obey in expectation received the blessing of the revelation of His mighty power among them. Every single person waiting in hope and expectation on Jesus was completely and fully satisfied. Even more is that they all watched as Jesus then asks his disciples to pick up the leftovers— not one ounce of the blessing to be wasted. When Jesus shows up, He shows up in love immeasurable, in power undeniable, with provisions unfathomable. Twelve baskets of leftovers— yes indeed, one for each disciple. What they witnessed and took part in was the result of the power of the Provider.

D. <u>Exaltation</u>: When the people had participated in the preparation and waited in expectation, they witnessed the most fantastic revelation and were left with one response— Exaltation! "This is indeed the Prophet who was sent into the world." The odd Truth here is, you get what you expect.

The crowd expected a Prophet to look like Jesus, but the Messiah would be something altogether different. At this point, the crowd acknowledged Jesus was from God but had not quite yet accepted the full Truth— that He was God. We see that Jesus left the crowd to avoid being exalted to the expected position of their own making. They saw His power, but their expectation of Messiah was so far off from reality. They couldn't see Him standing right in front of them. They acknowledged His might and gave Him a title of their choosing.

It is so essential that we prepare in the Truth of God's Word, know the Truth of His Word, and expect the Truth from God's Word so we can always be sure we are exalting the entirety of the Truth— the whole story of Jesus. We will share in exaltation only that which we've received in our time of preparation, according to our expectation, aligning with the level of our revelation. You may have to read that part again. It's quite the tongue twister, but loaded with goodies!

Remember also that not everyone will choose to sit down at the table with Jesus and be fed by His hand. Jesus met the need of those who were seated— those who accepted Him, obeyed Him, and expected Him to show up and reveal His glory.

So where are you in this story? Are you obedient in preparation? Waiting patiently upon Him in expectation? Amazed at His revelation? Making Him known in exaltation?

Or, are you content with self-effort— with a handful of loaves and fish? Are you content with living in need, always hungry for more, but looking around in defeat at your circumstances? You will receive according to your preparation and expectation. What are you expecting from Jesus today?

REALIGNMENT MUSINGS

1. Are you ready to do externally what God has been developing internally? For too many years it seemed the demands and expectations caused us to focus more on what was happening with the external, and it was not consistent with what was happening internally. We have to be careful and conscious about how we grow and live our lives, not promoting and propagating externally what we have not processed or developed internally. Otherwise, the "why" goes missing and the "what" gets muddled.

Here's an example— having good morals alone does not cause one to love. In fact, it can cause you to be judgmental. Love is what makes you all the things we are trying to be and do. It's easy to become too focused on behavioral modification at the expense of actual change (humility, brokenness, dependence, authentic community born out of love, etc.).

2. A major realignment for a healthy reframe can be seen here (Romans 5:3-5).

The way out of shame > hope!
The way to hope > character!

The way to character > perseverance!

The way to perseverance > trials / affliction / persecution!

3. We must stop chasing experiences! Our Christian culture seems to be obsessed with creating experiences for people. We see this in the marketplace, the church, and everywhere else. We can't give people Holy Spirit experiences. We can't program or teach experiences with a Holy God. Jesus did not give His life so we could have "cool" experiences. After spending a lot of time in Scripture, here is a common pattern we see in what we have affectionately called the great collision between God and man.

ENCOUNTER>EXCHANGE>EMPOWERED>EXPERIENCE

You see, if you start with a man-made experience, you will have a man moved encounter with the man alone— this leaves you empty and frustrated at best. Experience will never provide the encounter.

Encounter - One famous story you may know about from the Bible is in Acts 9. Paul (also known as Saul) encountered Jesus on his way to Damascus. This was not something he was seeking. In fact, just the opposite. Paul was a persecutor of Christians. Man could not have initiated this encounter. God initiates all encounters with Himself. Praise God for His encounter with us! When this encounter takes place, an exchange is necessary for us to follow Him.

Exchange - Using that same story of Paul's conversion in Acts 9, it's clear that his encounter with Jesus demanded an exchange. It's widely known that J. Hudson Taylor made the term "Exchanged Life" popular. You can read all about it in his book "Hudson Taylor's Spiritual Secret." The late and great Major W. Ian Thomas in his book "The Saving Life of Christ" speaks of this same principle. Thomas sheds significant light on the fact that it's not a shared life God is after, but an exchanged life— yours for His. Paul's exchange took time, involved other people, and was not easy. Two compelling passages conferencing the exchange are Matthew 16:24 and Mark 8:35.

33

Empowered - After an exchange like Paul had in Acts 9, we see a great work of God in and through Him. Verses 17-18 records this incredible filling and overflowing power of the Holy Spirit on and in Paul. Acts 1:8 says that we will receive power when the Holy Spirit comes on us. This is not just some random power for our good pleasure and personal experiences (which is what too many are after). This power is for a purpose. These purposes are where we find our ultimate experiences.

Experience - The workings of the Holy Spirit allow for the most incredible experiences. They can never be compared with those attempted by ourselves. Surely you can see why experiences are the byproduct and result of the encounter, exchange and empowering, right? The apostle Paul's conversion and transformation opened up the most amazing opportunities to experience the work of the Holy Spirit in and through His life. Now, if you have read much of the New Testament, you are aware that most of his experiences were painful, life-threatening, uninvited, full of heartache and headaches. Paul was grateful in the midst of all of them because they were experiences that made him more dependent on, and in love with Jesus! The warning here is, be careful not to chase experiences. They rarely look like the ones we see in the spotlights of many religious leaders, authors, churches and people's lives in general today.

Paul had such an effect on history and eternity. However, it started with his realignment. The same is true for us. To experience the fullness of Christ here on this planet, it will require a realignment.

READY FOR YOUR REALIGNMENT?

Recap: Realignment / Refocus

- What have you been trying to do on your own?
- What seems off to you? What will you do about it?
- What are you focused on that isn't consistent with the ways, the will and the Word of God?

Your Reframe needs a realignment, and the best way to do this is captured in Colossians 3:1-17. If you have a few minutes, check it out. This passage has the power to change your entire perspective on what it means to be in alignment with God in Christ by the power of the Holy Spirit!

After reading the Colossians passage, how do you think a realignment will change the way you encounter and experience the person of Jesus? Realistically? Practically?

SECTION 2

MAKING THE MAJOR REFRAMES

CHAPTER 5

THE BIBLE

THE WORD OF GOD!

John 1:1 (EXB) In the beginning [Gen. 1:1] ·there was the Word [the Word already existed; the Word refers to Christ, God's revelation of himself]. The Word was ·with [in the presence of; in intimate relationship with] God [the Father], and the Word was [fully] God.

What you believe about God's Word will determine everything else in your life for the rest of your life. This is why we're making this the first major reframe in this section. We'll get right to it here— is the Bible truth or not? Is it the truth, the whole truth, and nothing but the truth? Our goal here is to provide a small piece of perspective in hopes that no one would experience the effects of being destroyed by lack of knowledge (Hosea 4:6).

There are some common words used to describe The Holy

Bible. We will use many of them throughout this chapter (and the book as a whole). Here are some of them: God's Word; The Truth; Scriptures; Passages; The Bible. Everything starts with being better acquainted, intimately invested in the Bible. There are so many books, colleges, seminaries, professors, teachers, preachers, conferences, and workshops. With all that, we still had to learn to be good with knowing the Bible more than any other source, resource, expert, paradigm, model or method.

Once you plant your feet here, you will be catapulted into a passion for this living and active Word. Personal revival and true transformation becomes the fruit of your time in this living and active truth described here;

> *Hebrews 4:12 (NASB) For the Word of God is living and active and sharper than any two-edged sword, and piercing as far as the division of soul and spirit, of both joints and marrow, and able to judge the thoughts and intentions of the heart.*

This is where you will make or break your Reframe. Hebrews 4 says that all Scripture is inspired by God and useful for.... EVERYTHING!

We must make Scripture the most significant commentary to itself. Otherwise, we start misquoting and misrepresenting and misapplying it to our lives and the lives of others. You can actually relate and appreciate all that the Bible says without believing in your bones that God's Word is exactly that—from God and by God. If the Bible is truly from God, then it is by default inerrant, infallible and 100% accurate.

Giving yourself to the Word of God is very different than believing it from a distance. This is a crucial part of how we are transformed. Real transformation starts with God's Word. Fullness in Christ can't be experienced apart from it. Why is that? Because Jesus is the Word made flesh.

For us to be entirely open for learning Truth, there has to be at least a willingness to embrace two facts. The first is that our position may not always be 100% accurate. Next is, the Holy Spirit longs to reveal far more than we could ever imagine, learn, or retain (individually or collectively).

If you only know what you know, then how foolish to believe that what you know is all there is to know. Let's not be so naive as to assume that over the last few hundred years that a group of people that agreed on something affords us the right to believe we have "figured it out." God's relationship with humanity didn't come from or through Luther, Calvin, Graham, the Pope or any other person (other than Jesus).

There have been seismic shifts in the Christian Church caused by individuals obedience and disobedience to Truth (how Jesus referred to Himself in John 14:6). We have aligned the Word of God and the Spirit of God with man's understanding of God. Hence denominations, new age, new paradigms. Everything because of a man's interpretations.

When God revealed Himself to humans, they was never intended to create a following. That is still true today. Man in and of himself is never right. He is a man. He is dust (Psalm 103:14). Truth is only found in the person of Jesus by the revelation of the active work of the Holy Spirit. Far too many have taken their eyes off of God and have become impressed to follow a man instead of the God Who is leading the man. There's a term for that, and it's called idolatry.

Do you rely on God's Word alone for:

- Knowing and actively living your true **PURPOSE**? (Ephesians 2:10 / Proverbs 19:21)
- Acknowledging that He is your only true **PROVISION**? (John 3:27 / James 1:17)
- The source of your life's **PLANS**? (Jeremiah 29:11-14)
- Believing and embracing that all of the "yes and amen's" of your life are tied up in His **PROMISES**? (2 Corinthians 1:19-20)

The source is all according to His will, His purposes, and His glory. When we are in Christ, we are pleased. He is truly all we need, and we are satisfied. We don't seek pleasure from Christ as if He were a vendor. We find pleasure in Christ, the person, and we can be content in all circumstances. This is about us being genuinely fulfilled in who He is more than what He provides. One is about a personal relationship with Him, and the other seeks selfishly from Him. Only when we stop living for ourselves and find ourselves living in His incredible mercy and grace can we experience His purposes, provisions, plans, and promises. He's a good steward. He will wait for our surrender.

A few years ago a song came out that completely gripped us in every way possible, and became a passionate cry to the Lord for us. You may recognize the words from the great band, Mercy Me.

"Word of God Speak" -(Mercy Me)

I'm finding myself at a loss for words, and the funny thing is it's okay. The last thing I need is to be heard, but to hear what You would say.

Word of God speak, Would you pour down like rain. Washing my eyes to see Your majesty. To be still and know, that you're in this place. Please let me stay and rest in your holiness. Word of God speak

I'm finding myself in the midst of You, beyond the music, beyond the noise. All that I need is to be with You, and in the quiet hear Your voice

I'm finding myself at a loss for words, and the funny thing is it's okay.[6]

"*Sola Scriptura*" (Scripture alone or only)— Does that mean God does not speak and act outside of the words recorded in Scripture? Or, does it mean that God will never reveal something new to us that conflicts or competes with Scripture? For us, we see the Biblical evidence supporting the latter. Before you throw the book down, think about it this way— Since we know that all that happened in Jesus' life could not be contained or recorded in the Holy Scriptures, it stands to reason that just because those events and actions didn't make

6   Songwriters: Millard, Bart / Kipley, Pete, *Word of God Speak*, lyrics © Warner/Chappell Music, Inc, Essential Music Publishing, September 23, 2003.

the cut, they are still inspired and accurate. They would never conflict with the Word of God because they are still from the Son of God.

> *John 21:25 (TPT) Jesus did countless things that I haven't included here. And if every one of his works were written down and described one by one, I suppose that the world itself wouldn't have enough room to contain the books that would have to be written!*

God loves to reveal and display new things throughout history. Yes, even today! Scripture is replete with this very truth. When God reveals to us new things that are not recorded in Scripture, those things will never conflict with the Bible. In fact, just the opposite. They won't be standalone words but will bring to light that much more what is given us in the written Word of God. And, all things revealed will ultimately point to Jesus, give glory to God, demonstrate the power of the Holy Spirit and build up the church (Ephesians 4). I know it's scary for some of you reading this. There has been so much abuse of "the new" (which has been an issue since the beginning of the New Testament Church) for so long, and by so many. However, those abuses and misuses of truth cannot nullify the actual truth.

Take note— there is something incredibly important here in determining if something is from the Lord and consistent with the truth. Sound doctrine and grounded theology are critical (learning to divide the Word of Truth rightly). Paul told Timothy this truth;

> *2 Timothy 2:15 (GW) Do your best to present yourself to God as a tried-and-true worker who isn't ashamed to teach the word of truth correctly.*

The Gospel: There is no Gospel with an adjective in front of it (social, prosperity, etc.). However, God's Word addresses these issues in His Word. This is a significant difference and for some, an actual paradigm shift. It's so easy for us to get wrapped around the axle about specific, personal and social issues that are near and dear to our hearts. Learning to pull back from any one issue can provide a massive opportunity for a healthy reframe concerning receiving, living and teaching the fullness and wholeness of God's Word. This is why we must treat the Word of God as our sustenance and not supplemental. It's not a vitamin or energy drink. It's not for random parts of our life, interests, and passions. Remember, the Gospel is not just for salvation, but for ongoing restoration and sanctification.

On that note, have you asked yourself what you mean when you say "I want to be Biblical" or "I want to live according to the Bible?" Believing the God of the whole Bible is far more critical than believing and living according to the God of the New Testament. There are many Christians that dismiss the Old Testament as a history book full of allegories and stories to prove a point and is now antiquated, irrelevant or no longer necessary since Jesus has come. Friends, that could not be further from the truth.

It's apparent that people, in general, get bored with the truth. Why? What happens? People often say that they're searching for the truth in something or about something. This usually means they're doing a Google, TedTalk, Facebook, Instagram, Snapchat or Twitter search. Then, they talk to other people (equally flawed as they are). Finally, they consult their own emotions, common sense, logic and understanding (expansive I'm sure). Now they can sit on the high seat and cast their judgment and sentence on those who are not aligned with them. Paul addresses this with intensity in Romans 14:1-12. One particular verse should cause a moment of reflection and maybe a little bit of introspection.

> Romans 14:4 (ESV) says, Who are you to pass judgment on the servant of another? It is before his own master that he stands or falls. And he will be upheld, for the Lord is able to make him stand.

The Bible says if we really want to know the Truth, the Truth that actually has greater substance, the Truth we should be focusing on anyway, we can find it when we do this:

Jeremiah 29:12-13 (ESV) Then you will call upon Me and come and pray to Me, and I will hear you. You will seek Me and find Me, when you seek Me with all your heart.

A foundational and practical part of understanding God's Word is to see it through a relational lens. God is speaking to you as individual persons in addition to us as a people group. This makes much more sense when faced with the need for understanding our true condition. This is ultimately essential to someone going from death to life, lost to found, spiritually dead to alive in Christ. It's paramount in the salvation experience.

What are we talking about? The Bible says you were not born free. You can do nothing in your flesh to be free. Thus, you are enslaved to sin. Have that conversation over coffee at your next get-together. HA! This is ultimately what we are talking about. The Bible says every one of us was born enslaved to sin. God says that only Truth (Jesus) can set us free. But let's back up a little and break this down.

If we use John 8:31-59 as an example, we'll acquire a better understanding of Truth through the lens of the gospel. According to verses 31-32, living in the Truth is first, personal. Being in His Word is not about your family, your religious upbringing, your friends, etc. It's you being in intimate contact with Him. It's the way you see Him and understanding the way He sees you and listening to Him in those words written to you.

How many letters from someone have you read where you could hear their heart and voice through their written words? If you love to read books, you know how easy it is to get wrapped up in the words, partially because it can paint a picture that is as vibrant as reality itself. How much more so should this be true for us being wrapped up in THE WORD OF GOD?

Living in the Truth is both practical (life as a disciple) and personal. The Holy Spirit guides you in this Truth in practical ways. It's also powerful (seeing yourself as you are, and Jesus as He is). The Holy Spirit allows you to see yourself (and all that's going on with you) in light of Jesus, The Truth. Live in

His Word. Internalize it. Believe it. Receive it as your own for YOU, not just for someone else. Not for that person that you think needs to hear it. YOU need to hear it. Every single day. When we lose sight of this fact, we become overly preferential, self-righteous and judgmental— which is what we find in the people of Israel and the Jews in the temple in John 8:33-47.

Earlier in this passage, Jesus said that if they would believe in Him, abide in Him and His Word, they would be His disciples, know the Truth and be set free. The Jews answered with a somewhat delusional answer; "We have never been enslaved to anyone." Talk about not knowing the Word! Did anyone ever read the Old Testament (which is all the Jews had at the time)? The people of Israel were CONSTANTLY enslaved. Where had that truth gone over the years? And yet, when we fail to daily ingest God's Word for ourselves, on our own, and live and breathe it out daily, this is what we get! A kinder, gentler truth. Revised history. The truth that works in our favor. But make no mistake, partial truth is no truth at all. It is now poisoned with lies from the enemy that work to keep us from the REAL FREEDOM only found in the whole Truth of God's Word.

Listen, the Jews had access to it! They had the Torah. They could have seen and read and accepted for themselves the truth of their lineage— they were an enslaved people! They continually chose their way instead of God's. They added to God's commands by making up their own as well. They hardened their hearts and stiffened their necks. All the time! But they were blind to it. And again, your blind spots are only blind to you.

So the question that we would be wise to consider and answer is, do you believe what The Truth says about you? The alternative is to be a stiff-necked people, just as self-righteous as the Jewish nation— still living like you don't need the freedom that can only come from The Word.

It's noteworthy to mention that in John 8:34-38 the Jews were blinded to their condition which now Jesus uncovers in just one word— SIN. Jesus is gently and compassionately reminding them that yes, even their nation has a sin problem. He's revealing their true condition but in love. You struggle with sin, Israel. Therefore you are slaves to it. What sin did they struggle with? Well, how about murder? Oh, not in the physical realm just yet— but no sin begins in the physical realm. It starts with thoughts which move into your heart and become desires, which develops into your actions and become manifest physically. Jesus calls them out— YOU WANT TO KILL ME. Yeah, that might qualify as a sin issue! But what else can we draw out here?

If Jesus is THE TRUTH, He's ultimately saying; you don't like that I'm revealing your actual condition of sin and therefore, you want the Truth to die so your self-righteous version of yourself (who apparently doesn't need anything or anyone) can live. Rather than us dying to sin so Christ can reign in us, our flesh wants the Truth to die in us so that the flesh can reign. We ultimately love (in the flesh) relative truth and subjective truth. We love being the authors of our truth, or a version of it anyway.

Jesus also reveals the fact that slaves cannot free themselves. A slave could not just walk out of the Master's house and say, I'm done. I'm out of here. I've had it with serving, and I think I'll go live free now. No. Freedom has always been the Master's job, which was given to the Heir, the Son. Freedom is found only in the Son! And this my friends is The Gospel As The Truth.

A key point here in verse 37; Jesus knew of their righteous lineage as Jews, a chosen and beloved nation of the Father. He knew. He acknowledged this, "I know where you came from! I know who you were, but let me reveal who you are— you are enslaved to sin, and trying to kill me, the TRUTH... BECAUSE MY WORD FINDS NO PLACE IN YOU."

The Jewish people were steeped in tradition. They read the Torah. They taught the Torah. They recited the Torah. But somehow in the midst of it all, His Word found no place in them. It never took root! It never changed their hearts. It never changed their lives. Then Jesus gives a simple equation: You are a slave to sin because my Word has found no place in you.

What if your struggle today is pride, self-righteousness, envy, slander, malice, anger, lust, or jealousy? What if those struggles won't go away because the TRUTH about that sin, only found in God's Word, hasn't "found its place" in your heart? Could it be that you don't believe your particular struggle is sin? Could it be that you think "it's just the way you are?" And therefore, the rest of the world will remain subject to your struggle because you have no desire to change it? Truth can only find its place in us and transform us when we BELIEVE it, RECEIVE it, and LIVE it.

As their discussion continues in verses 39-42, Jesus continually says that if they were of Abraham, a faithful founding father, then they too would look like him. If we aren't modeling the values we profess, the Truth has found no place in us.

Then in verses 43-47 Jesus again gives the most simple equation for deafness toward God: "Why do you not understand what I say? It is because you cannot bear to hear MY WORD?" If we simply cannot (and therefore will not) tolerate what God shows us in the mirror of His Word, our actual condition, then we simply will remain deaf to the things of God. He follows again with another simple equation: Whoever is of God hears the words of God (verse 47). So which are you? Are you of God? Or are you of yourself and for yourself?

A choice has to be made. Do you believe what God says about your true condition? Or do you believe what YOU THINK about your true condition? We will always believe "we aren't that bad." We will compare ourselves to others. Social media provides the perfect outlet for you to compare and contrast yourself to find your "truth" every day. Surely you know all too well about the distorted truth of social media— right?

Do you believe what God's Word, the Truth, says about humanity? Do you believe that the heart of man (the old man, not the new you in Christ) is deceitful above all things? That your flesh will struggle with jealousy, envy, and strife? That as sons and daughters of God, you are not to quarrel and take part in petty discussions that lead to ungodliness? Do you believe that? Or do you think your brilliant thoughts and insights are worth sharing with everyone at all times, regardless of the outlet and irrespective of the audience? Do you press on whatever the issue or with little to no regard for the damage it can do to all those who have eyes to read and watch and ears to hear?

Lastly in verses 48-59, we have the ultimate showdown that we all face daily: Are we not right? Oh how we love to be right! It really fires us up and raises our blood pressure. It brings out the fighter in us. We love to be right! And yet, think about the revisionist history condition (we've never needed freedom, we've never been slaves to anything). This simply cannot coexist with the Truth of your condition— that apart from Christ you are enslaved to sin. And, that apart from abiding daily in His Word, the Truth will not be found in you. Therefore, you will never be free.

The Jews believed they were right. Jesus didn't appear as they wanted Him to. He didn't act how they wanted Him to act. He didn't say what they wanted Him to say. So they demonized Him. "He has a demon! He cannot be Truth, because we don't like it! Therefore, He must be a dark spirit, from the devil." Because surely, the Truth would only say things we agree with! The Truth would only tell us we're right. The Truth wouldn't ask us to change and see that we have sin that needs to be uprooted. No, that must be a crazy thought or some mysterious demon.

So we can mock the Jews, but could this be in the church today as well? The minute someone says or does something we don't approve of, something that ultimately is not our preference, we find our unique way to demonize them. We discover a way to distance ourselves. We find a way to prove our case why what we prefer is right and what they prefer is wrong. We make elaborate cases that could withstand any court of law, and draw our invisible lines in the sand. We're right. They're wrong. Let's take our proverbial ball from the playground and go home.

The Truth was right in front of them. However, their eyes were blinded by their preferences. The abiding truth of the Word had not found its place in them, and they refused to be set free. They were leaning on their own understanding rather than trusting in the Truth standing right before their eyes. They would not and could not accept that Jesus didn't meet their earthly criteria of a Messiah. He didn't behave in a Kingly fashion. He wasn't taking over nations with a scepter in hand. He was transforming hearts and changing the trajectory of lives instead. He was establishing His Kingdom and His will on earth.

Question: Will you choose to literally die on the hill of your preferred truth rather than live eternally by accepting the one and only Truth? Know this; it will often time mean you have to admit you're wrong. You will have to look in the mirror of His Word so you can be set free from the sin that binds you. You will have to realize that there are times you have gone at this Christian life thing all wrong.

When we abide in the Word, Jesus reveals Himself to us, and then we are set free as we realize who He is and who we are not. Will you believe and receive all He says about you in His word? Your true condition is that you desperately need Him every hour. He desires to mold you and shape you, changing your heart with Truth. Truth is the only way to Freedom. The Word is the only way to Truth. Notice we don't bring anything to the table for our freedom. It's all of God and from Him. Our gift! Will you let Jesus make true freedom your gift?

It's astonishing how many times we have been so easily misled. We don't want you to be deceived in anything. But know this, if you are looking to this world, your circle or yourself for the Truth of God's Word to be made real to you, you will be greatly disappointed. Part of the strengthening and increase in your defense against this is being grounded in sound doctrine. Tricky one here, doctrine. Let's take a quick second and address something we feel is quite important.

People and institutions have been arguing doctrine for quite some time. We are always grateful for scholars, wise counselors, theologians and the like. However, they are still people putting together the best they can doctrines of the Bible. Clearly, there are more beliefs called "doctrines" than what are actual doctrines in the Bible.

We should exercise caution when calling something a Biblical doctrine just because we feel strongly about it, or blindly follow someone else's definition or description of a doctrine. Be in the Word! Study it for yourself. Allow the work of the Holy Spirit to make it come alive to you! Be thankful for those who have worked and studied to provide for us these great writings. However, be like the Bereans— although they received the word from the apostles, they showed eagerness in examining the Scriptures for themselves (Acts 17:10-15). Now, let's talk more about doctrine for a few minutes.

<u>Doctrine</u>: A set of teachings/instructions that make up a system of belief and are embraced and taught as a way of life (our definition).

Does what you believe matter? Well, let's see if you have heard of any of these old wive's tales, myths, and misinterpreted/misused Scriptures:

- Cleanliness is next to godliness.
- God helps those who help themselves.
- If God is for us who can be against us (Ray Lewis).
- Feed a cold, starve a fever.
- Don't go outside with wet hair, you'll catch a cold.
- All we need is love, sweet love.
- Put Brandy on your baby's gums.
- If you love something, set it free. If it comes back it was meant to be.
- If you spill salt, throw some over your shoulder.
- All things work together for good… (Romans 8:28).
- I can do all things… (Philippians 4:13)
- Etc.

So why is doctrine so important? Your doctrine affects your faith which affects your trust. What you believe is fleshed out in how you trust. If you don't trust the ice to hold you, you will not have the faith to walk out onto it. Your faith is based on your trust. This is precisely what Paul begins with in his first letter to Timothy. In these six chapters, Paul is telling Timothy something fundamental. Make this distinction: there is a difference between educating someone and teaching/instructing them on how to apply it. Right? Paul's letters to Timothy and Titus are all about how to apply truth to individuals in the church and how to deal with those who are not solid in doctrine. So remember, Paul is not giving these churches (in this case the churches in Ephesus) new truth or new doctrine. He is teaching them how to apply it.

<u>Doctrine is important because</u>:

First: The Christian faith is based on one Truth, one Message— Jesus Christ died for our sins, was buried, then resurrected three days later and is alive today. In other words, the resurrection is real! (1 Corinthians 15:3-4 / Galatians 1:6-7)

Second: What you believe and ascribe to is what you teach and hand down. We must hold tightly to the trustworthiness of the Word! (Titus 1:9 / Genesis 18:19)

Third: It affects our life practically and eternally. The Bible in its entirety is breathed out by God and useful for all areas of faith and life. (Revelation 22:18-19 / 2 Timothy 3:16 / John 8:31-32 / Romans 12:2 / Psalm 119:165)

We are called and commissioned to be faithful soldiers fighting for the faith. If we have no sound doctrine, we have no fight for an authentic faith. We want to be able to echo Paul's words in his second letter to Timothy; *2 Timothy 4:7 (ESV) I have fought the good fight, I have finished the race, I have kept the faith.*

WHAT ABOUT YOU?

Think about it— do you really believe the Bible? How would you know? How would others know that you believe the Bible? How is it changing your life practically?

Here's a couple questions to consider:

1. Are you living the lessons personally that you're willing to give others?

2. Do you believe and receive the same as you teach and tell?

Remember, emphasis on an issue in scripture without it being in the context of the whole story or teaching leads to a bad reframe and inaccurate picture. You'll create your own picture from it. Are doctrines important? Of course they are. However, doctrines aren't the message. They support the message. They are more about keeping us connected to the main message (discussed more in chapter 11).

This Truth has a purpose. It's to set you free. Are you ready to be free? Are you ready for this amazing living and breathing Word of God to continue changing your life? Take a deeper look at Hebrews 4:12-13. If you believe this Word is as powerful as God claims, then how is it impacting your life practically in relation to 2 Timothy 3:16-17?

For further study on what the Bible has to say about, well, the Bible, check these passages out:

1 Corinthians 15:3-4 / Galatians 1:6-7 / Titus 1:9 / Genesis 18:19 / Revelation 22:18-19 / 2 Timothy 3:16-17 / John 8:31-32 / Romans 12:2 / Psalm 119:165

CHAPTER 6

THE TRIUNE GOD

FATHER, SON, HOLY SPIRIT.

Alan Hirsch shares in a video about being careful in how we are seeking God. He says that our perception and understanding of God determines who we are pursuing. So be careful and get it right or we will pursue a false god or a misrepresentation of the true God. The same goes for the rest of the Triune God (The Son and Holy Spirit).[7]

Much teaching is offered about God (although not always accurate and/or complete). We want to point out that we will use the following words and phrases synonymously; Trinity, Triune God, and The Godhead. More than a theology lesson, this is more about our relationship not just with the Godhead, but with each "person" within it.

So many church-goers may know a little about God the Father and the Son. We want to share part of the reframe we

---

7   Hirsch, Alan, *"The Danger of Seeking God,"* www.exploregod.com., retrieved March 18, 2018, https://www.exploregod.com/the-danger-of-seeking-god-video.

received concerning the Father in this chapter. However, there are two chapters in this book that speak much of Jesus and His attributes, purpose, and place in the Trinity. Consequently, we'll say very little about Jesus in this section. The majority of this chapter focuses on what we understand to be the right approach concerning the Holy Spirit. "Right approach" is the key verbiage here. Not total. Not singular. Not most importantly. Alright— let's start with God, our Father.

GOD - THE FATHER

It's sad beyond words the number of incomplete and unhealthy ways people view God the Father. So many undervalue Him and see Him as their cosmic buddy. Many see Him as their cosmic killjoy. Too many people walk around afraid (which is not exactly the same as fearing God) that He is looking for ways to crush them. We have seen this lead to performance anxiety, shame, guilt, and fear of messing up. We often watched people confuse holiness with simply working hard. This almost always causes unnecessary hardships as well as missing the loving heart of God altogether.

Incredibly, God has given us the imagery of a father so we can better understand His heart and love for us as our Heavenly Father. However, there are so many that did not grow up with fathers that carry those same attributes. Some fathers did some downright hurtful and hateful things to their kids. For them, referring to God as their "Father" may not be received and appreciated initially the same as other Christians with better experiences.

There are so many personal examples we could give in regards to how the Father has shown Himself to us. Instead, let's check out how some of the ways God the Father reveals Himself in the Bible.

He is Spirit and person but not a human (Number 23:19, John 4:24). He is love (1 John 4:8). He created all things (Genesis 1:1, Colossians 1:16). He is a loving Father who calls us His children (1 John 3:1-24). He is merciful (Deuteronomy 4:31). He loves us so much He sent His Son Jesus to die for our sins (John 3:16). He strengthens us and helps us (Isaiah 41:10)

Maybe you have your favorites as well. We encourage you to spend some quality time looking through the Bible and discovering how amazing our Heavenly Father is. He is so unique in the way He can be both a wrathful Judge and a tenderhearted Love. He can be and do all this at the same time with complete perfection. He is gentle, and a mighty warrior. He speaks with all authority and is the most sensitive listener. He does all of this with completeness, fullness, lacking in nothing, and with sovereign power and authority. Wow! Our Father truly is amazing, loving, and worthy of believing, knowing, trusting, and following.

GOD - THE SON

Make no mistake, when God sent His Son, Jesus to live and die and ascend back into heaven, this was no small sacrifice. Jesus, the perfect Son of God, gave up so much to provide an opportunity for us to have a right relationship with God the Father. This was a necessary decision from the courts of heaven for God to have a relationship with man after the fall in Genesis 3. But there is more to Jesus as the Son than the way we understand sons here on earth.

Depending on the type of church you grew up in or attend even now, you might remember the simple song, "There's Something About That Name." See if these lyrics connect with you the way they do with us.

> *Jesus, Jesus, Jesus; there's just something about that name.*
>
> *Master, Savior, Jesus, like the fragrance after the rain;*
>
> *Jesus, Jesus, Jesus, let all Heaven and earth proclaim*
>
> *Kings and kingdoms will all pass away,*
>
> *But there's something about that name.*
>
> *Kings and kingdoms will all pass away,*
>
> *But there's something about that name.*[8]

---

8   Gaither, Bill, Gaither, Gloria, "There's Something About That Name," CAPITOL CHRISTIAN MUSIC GROUP, © 1970 William J. Gaither.

Jesus, the Son of God! His name alone changes things. His name alone causes the demons to tremble in terror (James 2:19). There truly is something about that name. A proper reframe concerning the person of Jesus Christ is critical beyond words. Look at some places here in the Bible that reveal Jesus, the Son of God:

- He is the Way, Truth, and the Life (John 14:6)
- He is the Word of God (John 1:1, 14)
- He guarantees no condemnation for those who are a part of Him (Romans 8:1)
- He came to seek and save the lost (Luke 19:10)
- He is the only way to salvation (Acts 4:12, John 3:16)
- He is called Wonderful Counselor, Mighty God, Everlasting Father, Prince of Peace (Isaiah 9:6)

Seriously, there are not enough pages in the world to contain all the names, characteristics, and attributes of Jesus. Think about some of the ways Jesus has shown Himself to you. Reflect on those places in the Bible that display the splendor of our King Jesus! He is undoubtedly worthy of your worship and praise.

God - The Holy Spirit

What if we started our kids out with how to listen and discern the Holy Spirit? Or how to test things Biblically in the Spirit? Even how to be led and governed by the work of the Holy Spirit? For those who had this privilege, you are blessed and fortunate. However, many of us grew up in a faith system that didn't spend a lot of time talking about the Person, Power, and Presence of the Holy Spirit.

The more we experienced personally and witnessed, the more we began to ask "What's the deal with the Holy Spirit?" We found faithful and trustworthy followers of Jesus that had a much more intimate relationship with the Holy Spirit than we had ever known possible. They were gracious, patient, and incredible resources as we learned and experienced a more biblically authentic relationship with the Holy Spirit.

The work and power of the Holy Spirit are to equip and empower us to be both disciples and disciple-makers of Jesus— bringing glory to God and strength to His church. The focus is still Jesus. We're not disciples of the Holy Spirit. We're disciples of Jesus Christ. For Him. From Him. Through Him. So let's see what a this reframe regarding the Holy Spirit looks like.

Reframe - Being filled with the Holy Spirit.

This is a doctrine and subject that has caused quite a division amongst Christians. We would need more than a chapter to dive into this at a deeper level. We want you to know that our goal here isn't persuading you towards a particular side. It's just the opposite. There is much more to the workings of the Holy Spirit than any one party or camp can contain or conquer. Our goal is to challenge you to listen to the Holy Spirit in a way that is consistent with Scripture and not champion the stance of any particular group or pre-packaged paradigm.

Here are some things we know for certain about the Holy Spirit (mainly because it's what the Bible says):

- He empowers us to be witnesses of Jesus Christ (Acts 1:8)
- He dwells in us as the new temple (1 Corinthians 6:19)
- He is a gift given to us at salvation (Acts 2:38)
- He teaches us all things pertaining to God (John 14:26, 1 Corinthians 2:13)
- He bears fruit in us (Galatians 5:22-23)
- He helps us even when we don't know what to say (Romans 8:26)

The Holy Spirit takes up residence with us and in us. We are heart, soul, body, and mind (Luke 10:27). The Spirit of God takes up residency with us the moment we become believers and followers of Jesus. Once that happens, we have this access to the heart, thoughts, and ways of God. All of this because of the Holy Spirit. Otherwise, we cannot know these things (1 Corinthians 2:11).

Ephesians 5:15-21 speaks of being filled with the Holy Spirit instead of being drunk on wine. This is a great contrast given us here. Author and Pastor J.D. Greear preached a message from this text on being filled with the Holy Spirit. He gave a short but sweet contrast here;

> "But there's a crucial difference between being filled with alcohol and being filled with the Spirit. Alcohol changes a person's perception by deadening him to reality; the Spirit changes a person's perception by awakening him to reality. When we are filled with the Spirit, we are not numbed to the pains of the world, but our eyes are opened to God's beauty and power. When Elisha's servant's eyes were opened, he did not see a smaller Syrian army, but angels with swords in chariots of fire that dwarfed the Syrian force (2 Kings 6:17). When Paul was filled with the Spirit the pain did not go away, his eyes were opened to comfort and joy greater than his pain (2 Corinthians 6:9-10)."[9]

There is a supernatural power released in us and through us when we are filled with the Holy Spirit. It will always be for a purpose. There is room for no other agenda, purpose or person. Our love and loyalty are all bound up in Him. We are filled not for our own experiences and enjoyment, but for the profound and straightforward purpose of knowing Jesus and making Him known— to love Him supremely and others sacrificially (The Great Commandment - Luke 10:27).

Part of the work of the Holy Spirit is to empower us to be His (Jesus') witnesses in Jerusalem, Judea, Samaria and the rest of the world. Well, since most readers do not live in

9   Greear, J.D., "Filled With The Holy Spirit: What, When, and How," www.churchleaders.com, March 22, 2012, retrieved August 13, 2014, https://churchleaders.com/outreach-missions/outreach-missions-blogs/159906-jd_greear_filled_with_the_holy_spirit_what_when_and_how.html.

those regions, what does that mean? They were to go out where they were (Jerusalem), their home towns or current residences. Then, keep going until you can't go any further. In today's economy, and with our advanced technology and transportations choices, we can go everywhere any time. However, don't neglect where you are in order to go where you're not (yet).

Have you ever heard the song "Holy Spirit?" Well, this was the moment it all changed for us. No, really. Let us explain. I (Clay) had just returned from a trip to Tibet with my son and some very close friends. During that trip I was exposed to the power of the Holy Spirit in ways that forever changed me. I could no longer deny and brush off so many of the stories I had from people throughout the years, and out of fear couldn't quite believe. It wasn't their stories that was so hard for me to believe. Down deep, my struggle was whether or not I believed the Holy Spirit still moved like that today. The fight was real. Here are the words to that song that resonated with me as a result of my time in Tibet:

HOLY SPIRIT

There's nothing worth more, that could ever come close

No thing can compare, You're our living hope

Your presence, Lord

I've tasted and seen, of the sweetest of loves

Where my heart becomes free, and my shame is undone

Your presence, Lord

[Chorus:]

Holy Spirit, You are welcome here

Come flood this place and fill the atmosphere

Your glory, God, is what our hearts long for

To be overcome by Your presence, Lord

Your presence, Lord

Let us become more aware of Your presence
Let us experience the glory of Your goodness[10]

We know there is potential for unhealthy doctrine here. The Holy Spirit is everywhere. He doesn't necessarily need to be invited into somewhere He already is. The invitation is not for His benefit, but ours. It's more of a response to His invitation. But He won't barge in and create relationship and intimacy with you— hence the invitation.

Who is the Holy Spirit and what does He do? This is one of the most important and frequently asked questions from followers of Christ. Let's take some time and work through this. First, we read in John 14:16-17, 26-27 that Jesus would leave for all His followers the Holy Spirit. And, the Holy Spirit would empower them, befriend them, set them free, teach them all things in Jesus' name, and inspire them to remember or recount everything that Jesus had taught them. This is all part of the reframe God desires for you regarding the Holy Spirit.

Part of the confusion with the Holy Spirit for many people is knowing how to refer to Him. Is the Holy Spirit just an essence? Force? Representation of God? Idea or theory? According to Lifeway Research, 56% of evangelical Christians believe the Holy Spirit is not a person, but a force. Francis Chan dives deeper into this in his book, "Forgotten God." Great book— check it out. Here is a great perspective from R.C. Sproul:

> The fact that the Holy Spirit is a person is seen in a multitude of ways in Scripture. One of the primary evidences is that the Bible repeatedly and consistently uses personal pronouns to refer to Him. He is called "He," "Him," and so on, not "it." But the Holy Spirit is seen in Scripture not merely as personal but also as fully divine.[11]

10   Torwalt, Katie, Wilson , Bryan Andrew, "Holy Spirit," Capitol Christian Music Group, 2011.
11   Sproul, R. C., "*Who Is the Holy Spirit,?*" Vol. 13, p. 10, Orlando, FL, Reformation Trust, 2012.

John 16:5-7 describes the Holy Spirit as the Helper and Advocate. The umbrella description for the Holy Spirit in the Greek is this; "parakletos" [par·ak·lay·tos] - called to one's aid or side (one who pleads another's cause before a judge; a pleader, counsel for defense; legal assistant; an advocate; one who pleads another's cause with one; an intercessor.[12]

Also, He does things that we associate with personality. He teaches, inspires, guides, leads, grieves, convicts us regarding sin, and more. Impersonal objects do not behave in this manner. Only a person can do these things.

He speaks to those who are far from Him (Conviction). John 16:8-11 describes The Holy Spirit as the One who speaks to us:

Concerning SIN

hamartia [ham·ar·tee·ah] - missing the mark; failure; offense; wrongdoing; choosing the wrong course.

Concerning RIGHTEOUSNESS

dikaiosune [dik·ah·yos·oo·nay] - the condition acceptable to God.

Concerning JUDGEMENT

krisis [kree·sis] - decision or verdict; crisis— a time when an important decision must be made.

He is described as a Helper because while our call is to go into all the world, it is HIS job to bring conviction to the world. A conviction has to come from a judge, and since there is none righteous, not one (Romans 3:10, Psalm 14:1-3, 53:1-3), we are exempt from having a seat on the Judge's bench.

God has created every person that is living far from Him and in denial of Him. He loves them. He has ordained their path and ordered their steps. His role reminds us what ours

---

12   Strong's Definitions, *parakletos* definition, www.blueletterbible.org, retrieved February 9, 2019, https://www.blueletterbible.org/lang/lexicon/lexicon.cfm?t=kjv&strongs=g3875.

is not. Only the Holy Spirit brings change to the souls of men. What if we stopped trying to sentence the world and started telling them how much God loves them and desires that none should perish?

We also read that He speaks to those who belong to Him (the redeemed) in a unique and personal way. This is painted perfectly for us in John 16:12-15. This passage says it is The Holy Spirit that guides you into all the truth by communicating with God and revealing those conversations to you. We often say God is Love. And, this is true. And in the same manner, Jesus is Truth. Jesus speaks the truth— all truth past, present, and even the future. He does this through The Holy Spirit, who then reveals this truth to us.

Just as the Holy Spirit is the only One who can communicate the reality of the lost persons' circumstance to them, He is also the only One who can reveal the truth of our present situations to us. We can at best see dimly, in part. But the Holy Spirit has access to the fullness of all wisdom and knowledge of heaven— He sees ALL the truth. He can give us the wisdom, insight, and confidence to move into whatever our future may hold. We cannot have access to all truth without the Spirit of God. We cannot have access to things to come without the Spirit of God. This role belongs only to Him, and anything less is just the musings of man.

In John 16:14, the Holy Spirit's goal is forever and always to glorify the Father. The One who can guide us into all truth is also the One who can help us bring all glory to God here on earth. The Holy Spirit takes all that belongs to Jesus and imparts it to the children of God. He serves as the holy interpreter, using the many gifts of God within the body of Christ. The Father is perfect in all wisdom, understanding, strategies, plans, solutions, healing, the advancement of His kingdom, etc. The Holy Spirit is the one moving in us to reach toward heaven and pray down the things of the Father here on earth. He is the key to bringing His Father's kingdom to earth. He is the key to giving us the love and the language we need to reach all the lost kids out there— those created by God who are wayward, misled and dying. The Holy Spirit is the key to knowing how to love and serve each other with all love, wisdom, and discernment.

God, our Father, loves us and reaches out to us through

God the Son, Savior, and Redeemer. God the Holy Spirit convicts and convinces us of the Father's love, authority and power over our sin, and inevitable death and destruction. It is the Holy Spirit that makes a way in our heart and mind to both receive and respond to this unmatchable act of love, grace, and mercy. We have a part to play in all of this. We will respond in one way or another.

Side note: don't feel bad about the fact that there is no way you will be able to completely wrap your minds around these deep and profound roles, responsibilities, and attributes. However, we do praise God that He has made known to us all that we can receive, process, believe, and live out.

A proper reframe can position us to call out to Him more effectively. The following are passages that can truly open your eyes. Remember, He truly desires you to see, hear, know, and experience Him in the most amazing ways.

> *Jeremiah 33:3 (ESV) Call to me and I will answer you, and will tell you great and hidden things that you have not known.*
>
> *Psalm 139:17-18 (ESV) How precious to me are your thoughts, O God! How vast is the sum of them! If I would count them, they are more than the sand. I awake, and I am still with you.*

Hearing from the Holy Spirit is NOT reserved for the ones that are doing it all "correctly." Why? Because if that's the case, it's a system and process driven by works-related and human-made efforts that cause God to speak on demand. So why walk by the Spirit? The short answer— depth and breadth with the Savior and intimacy with your Father in Heaven. All your core and actual needs and desires are found here.

There is a filling and fulfilling that you receive only in the context of intimacy. Access to knowledge is made known only in the context of right relationship. Peace and ultimate fulfillment are experienced only to the degree we walk in surrender and obedience to Jesus.

It's not just a matter of calling out to Him. We must start listening better. Pay attention to the ordinary things in your day that happens right in front of you. He is always speaking.

To whom are you attributing what you hear? Sometimes we struggle if God is speaking to us through the Holy Spirit. Know this; He is always speaking (in one way or another).

> *Job 33:13-18 (ESV) 13 Why do you contend against him, saying, "He will answer none of man's words? 14 For God speaks in one way, and in two, though man does not perceive it. 15 In a dream, in a vision of the night, when deep sleep falls on men, while they slumber on their beds, 16 then he opens the ears of men and terrifies them with warnings, 17 that he may turn man aside from his deed and conceal pride from a man; 18 he keeps back his soul from the pit, his life from perishing by the sword.*

Have you seen how the Holy Spirit speaks through circumstances (good and bad), nature (all of it), movies & music (the arts) and a myriad of other ways? It's extraordinary!

We can't express how important it is to respond in this way— OBEDIENCE! It's not enough to sense Him, listen to Him, believe Him, and talk about Him. We must obey Him! Below is one such area of obedience often ignored or rebelled against.

> *Acts 1:8 (TPT) But I promise you this—the Holy Spirit will come upon you and you will be filled with power. And you will be my messengers to Jerusalem, throughout Judea, the distant provinces—even to the remotest places on earth!*

When we operate in this reality, everything changes. Everything! When we seek, listen and obey the Holy Spirit, it all changes. We have direction and purpose. We walk in His promises. And, we have all the provisions necessary for any place He takes us. The opposite of obeying the Holy Spirit is to grieve the Holy Spirit. We grieve the Spirit when we sin. John 17 describes how the Holy Spirit is all about unity. So, it should not be hard to understand why it grieves His heart when there is discord amongst believers. And, woe to the one(s) who would instigate it (Proverbs 6:16-19).

In our experience, there are too many churches off of center— not because of their view of man, but their opinions and beliefs of the Holy Spirit regarding who He is and what He does. So the mind of radical fundamentalism remains darkened in their understanding. This all too familiar mindset and paradigm causes many to lose out on the full and intended work of the Spirit. This often leads to missing the entire work of the Word in and through their life as well.

Part of the danger with all this is how easy it is to compartmentalize the Spirit to align with our structure rather than submitting our internal and external structure to the will and design of the Holy Spirit. As the dominoes fall, reductionism (reducing the extraordinary to the ordinary) is the next logical consequence. As a result of this faulty understanding, people will hurt people. And, the cycle continues.

Conversely (to radical fundamentalism), those who express their faith exclusively through the stereotype of "hyper-charismatic," will focus primarily on the supernatural workings of the Spirit and do not submit themselves to the Word (having good theology and doctrine) as they should. The tendency is to pick only the stories and passages from the Bible that speak of the supernatural, the gifts, etc. Once again, this places too much emphasis on any one of the persons of the Godhead and can cause a form of darkness in understanding. Once again, this can become harmful to the whole body.

This is part of the struggle in many denominational constructs. They've chosen an emphasis rather than a fullness— man's work and structures versus letting the Holy Spirit work in their hearts. The Holy Spirit now has to break through the trap of our processes and plans so that God's Word can be as life-changing and straightforward as it was intended.

Man wants to try and take responsibility for the spiritual development of man. The truth is, apart from the active work of the Spirit, we are only providing more religious hoops to jump through, and more processes and programs to subscribe to. These are hollow and unfortunately, end up serving as traps. Once again, the Holy Spirit has to break through these structures to reach the heart of man. Only this brings real change to their hearts and minds.

It's shocking how much of His role and responsibilities we try and do on our own. Ultimately, we are saying we don't trust the Holy Spirit is powerful enough or desires enough to grow and develop people. Friends, this is not our responsibility. It's unfathomable how we've made a multi-million dollar industry of it. We have all the books, curriculum, programs and plans to develop Christians into maturity (so we think). True life change happens only as a result of a direct encounter with Jesus through a powerful encounter with the Holy Spirit. It will never be from a great sermon or a new class (although God can use these supplementally for our development). It will be the presence of the Holy Spirit that changes lives. Why would we ever want to attempt to reproduce this as mere mortals? The Holy Spirit changes lives. Man serves as nothing more than a stumbling block when we point to wisdom and structures built of man.

Isaiah 2:22 (ESV) Stop regarding man in whose nostrils is breath, for of what account is he?

Let's start wrapping up this chapter with these words from R.A. Torrey:

Do we know the "communion of the Holy Ghost?" (2 Corinthians 13:14). Communion means fellowship, partnership, comradeship. Do we know this personal fellowship, this partnership, this comradeship, this intimate friendship, of the Holy Spirit? Herein lies the secret of a real Christian life, a life of liberty and joy and power and fullness. To have as one's ever-present Friend, and to be conscious that one has as his ever-present Friend, the Holy Spirit, and to surrender one's life in all its departments entirely to His control, this is true Christian living.[13]

---

13   Torrey, R. A., *"The Fundamentals: A Testimony to the Truth,"* (Kindle Locations 11730-11736). www.DelmarvaPublications.com. Kindle Edition, Published June 20, 2013.

Remember, this is in no way an exhaustive study on the Triune God. It's probably safe to say that all the books that have ever been written could not together even begin to scrape the surface of the depths of the Father, Son, and Holy Spirit. The purpose of this reframe is to stir in you a desire for a more profound love and excitement to know and commune with the Triune God! Maybe there is more to them than you've been taught. Perhaps there are areas of your doctrinal position that need to be broadened, realigned, corrected or even challenged. Whatever the case, our prayer is that you seek to know all three of the Godhead in a way you never have before- and never stop!

Daniel Henderson has done a great job giving us a fantastic challenge regarding the way we think and speak concerning the Holy Spirit. Here are a few from his list:

> *INSTEAD OF*: "We just want to soak in the Holy Spirit."
>
> *HOW ABOUT*: "Lord, enable us to honor and obey the indwelling Holy Spirit."
>
> *INSTEAD OF*: "The Holy Spirit came."
>
> *HOW ABOUT*: "The Holy Spirit worked powerfully in our lives."
>
> *INSTEAD OF*: "Holy Spirit, fall."
>
> *HOW ABOUT*: "Holy Spirit, fill, control, and dominate our lives."
>
> *INSTEAD OF*: "Pour out Your Spirit."
>
> *HOW ABOUT*: "Spirit, take charge of our lives."
>
> *INSTEAD OF*: "God showed up."
>
> *HOW ABOUT*: "The Spirit worked powerfully in us and among us."

INSTEAD OF: "The atmosphere is changing."

HOW ABOUT: "The Holy Spirit is working in us to change us."

INSTEAD OF: "Let Your glory fall."

HOW ABOUT: "Jesus, You are our glory. We seek Your will and word."

INSTEAD OF: "Rain down on us."

HOW ABOUT: "Take control of our hearts by Your indwelling Spirit."[14]

---

14   Henderson, Brad, *"I'm Not Dead and the Holy Spirit is Not a Force,"* www.strategicrenewal.com, 2018, retrieved February 2019, https://www. strategicrenewal.com/2018/06/04/im-not-dead-and-the-holy-spirit-is-not-a-force/.

WRAPPING YOUR HEAD AROUND IT!

It sounds impossible to completely wrap your head around the mystery of the Triune God / Godhead / Trinity. We have good news for you; you will never completely understand this mystery in its fullness until Jesus returns. However, we have been given the Word of God and the Holy Spirit who teaches us everything we need to know in order to believe, obey, and follow Him. We encourage you to seek the Truth already revealed to you through His Word and through the relationship you have already been given in Christ.

Brad Jersak provides some practical ways the Holy Spirit can speak to you. Take a minute and consider how God can talk to you through these means.

Scripture: Has God ever spoken to you through his Word? Ask him what book he would like you to read from today. Ask him to highlight a verse that will nourish your soul. As you read, take note of any phrases that jump out at you. Ask God why he wants you to know that.

Conviction: Has God ever pointed out sins for which you needed to seek forgiveness from God or others? Ask God if you've grieved his heart this week in any way. Ask him if he would forgive you. Does he ever affirm areas in you that truly please him? Ask him to show you some.

Burdens: Has God ever brought people to mind for prayer? Ask God to give you the name or show you the face of someone he wants you to pray for today. How does he see and feel about that person? How would he like to bless him or her? Release that blessing in prayer.

Prompting: Has God ever prompted you to share something with someone? Ask God to help you compose a written prayer of blessing for someone you know well.[15]

15   Jersak, Brad, "*Can You Hear Me? Tuning in to the God who Speaks,*" (Kindle Locations 940-967), Partial List, Fresh Wind Press, Brad Jersak, 2012.

CHAPTER 7

IT'S PERSONAL

LOOK AT YOU!

LET'S TALK ABOUT YOU!

Let's start with some big questions that you might need to deal with before you can experience a reframe in the area of identity. Are you the total sum of your jobs, paychecks, savings and investments, trophies and placards, acknowledgments, etc.?

When someone asks who you are, they're usually asking you what you do. The question is "who writes your paychecks?" Or, "Who do you work for?" And, it is surmised that this is who you are. Well, that would mean that if you are not drawing a steady paycheck with a company logo on it, then you're less than the rest of the hard working citizens around you. And, somehow this is your fault, and you should probably do something about it. Why? Because your identity is at stake.

By the way, the same can happen within a marriage or circle of friends. We have experienced and seen how much struggle there can be in marriage when you're trying to find too much of your identity in and from each other. As a husband or wife, are you only what you perceive the other to think about you? As a spouse, are you living up to the perceived value the other is placing on you? If not, what does that make you? See? It gets all kinds of crazy up in here with marriage and identity.

For us to have a strong understanding of who we are, our true identity, we need to start with the Author and Maker of that very identity. Check out what God has to say about you in His Word.

Matthew 5 says that you are the salt of the earth, a light in the world. Matthew 28 says that you are a disciple-maker. John 15 says that you are an intimate friend of Jesus. 1 Corinthians 6 says that you have the Holy Spirit living in you. 2 Corinthians 5 says that you are a new person. Galatians 3 says that you are a son or daughter of God. Ephesians 2 says that you are a work of art. Philippians 3 says that you are a citizen of Heaven.

Of course, the list goes on and on. What do any or all of these passages say about you as a believer and follower of Christ? Do you still need more help with who you are? Need more convincing and clarity? Maybe try working your way through the New Testament with a friend and explore just how much you are loved and treasured!

2 Corinthians 5:17 makes it clear that you are in Christ; you are a new creation! New in Christ means that your former identity is gone. OK, then why is that so hard to grasp? Why can't you live in that reality more and more? Why do you let your fear create such a warped and false sense of identity?

What if you realized that you already have all you need within you because of the work of Jesus in and through you? You are a chosen child of God! You are not alone. In Christ, you are enough (your sufficiency is due to His sufficiency) to the Father. Let's take a closer look at what causes some of our identity crises.

We want to start by expressing how our heart hurts for those who struggle with mental and/or emotional challenges and disease. In some ways, some of these challenges allow us to understand better the problems found in the church. As we looked into some of these emotional and mental challenges, we noticed some similar characteristics on a spiritual level within the body of Christ today. Here are just a few of those parallels including the definition, and how we see them manifested on a spiritual level:

I. BI-POLAR

"Bipolar disorder, formerly called manic depression, is a mental health condition that causes extreme mood swings that include emotional highs (mania or hypomania) and lows (depression)."[16]

In the same body and with the same mind of Christ, we can be so divided. And, you never know who is going to show up to the party. Is it the one who is entirely on board, surrendered to the Spirit of God, and bringing blessing to the body with every step? Or, is it the one who comes in with anger, slander, and dishonor on their lips? The one firmly planted on the judgment seat, full of a critical and divisive spirit? Clearly, Christ does not desire this bipolar nature to His bride.

James 3:10-12 (ESV) From the same mouth come blessing and cursing. My brothers, these things ought not tone so. Does a spring pour forth from the same opening both fresh and salt water? Can a fig tree, my brothers, bear olives, or a grapevine produce figs? Neither can a salt pond yield fresh water.

Know this— a tree is known by its fruit. And we are all daily bearing the fruit of the flesh or the fruit of the spirit. We cannot fool those around us forever. Our tree will bear what springs up from inside us. The question is, have we nurtured and fed the flesh, or the Spirit (Romans 8, Galatians 5)?

---

16   Mayo Clinic, "Bipolar Disorder," overview, www.mayoclinic.org, retrieved October, 2018, https://www.mayoclinic.org/diseases-conditions/bipolar-disorder/symptoms-causes/syc-20355955.

II. ANXIETY

"Experiencing occasional anxiety is a normal part of life. However, people with anxiety disorders frequently have intense, excessive and persistent worry and fear about everyday situations. Often, anxiety disorders involve repeated episodes of sudden feelings of severe anxiety and fear or terror that reach a peak within minutes (panic attacks)."[17]

Anxiety is the buzz word of the century. Oh to have been on the front end of the pharmaceutical industry when anxiety meds came to town! Yikes. Anxiety is here, there and everywhere. In our homes, in our churches, in our schools, in our workplace. Everyone is anxious, nervous, and worrying. About everyone. And everything. Everywhere.

But why? Why is the bride so plagued with this fear and anxiety? What does the bride fear the most? Ultimately, it's safe to assume that most brides would fear not being provided for by their husband (in whatever ways they are expecting). She would fear putting her future in another person's hands. She would fear not knowing where the future would take her. Let's call this out for what is truly is. The bride has a trust issue. The bride does not trust her Groom.

So, brothers and sisters, do we truly trust in the Lord with all our heart? And, are we choosing to not lean on our own understanding (Proverbs 3:5-7)? Are we following the command, not suggestion, of Jesus to not worry about tomorrow because we've got plenty to handle on our own plate for today (Matthew 6:34)? Do we genuinely believe our groom when He says we are more valuable to Him than the beautifully clothed lilies of the field, and more dear to Him than the sparrows that he feeds? Do we believe that He truly is the God Who Sees and that He knows our every need in every circumstance? Do we believe Him when He says He is *Jehovah-Jireh*, The Lord Will Provide? Do we know and

17   Mayo Clinic, "Anxiety Disorders," overview, www.mayoclinic.org, retrieved October, 2018, https://www.mayoclinic.org/diseases-conditions/anxiety/symptoms-causes/syc-20350961.

understand that if He wanted to sustain us by food from ravens and water from the rock (1 Kings 17:2-16), He is still fully capable and could do so at any given moment?

What do we genuinely absorb in our inner being about the goodness of our Father? What rock will we stand upon when the storms rage? Jesus has promised He will never leave us or forsake us. Do we trust in Him? Or, to circle back to Forecasting from an earlier chapter, have we already written the future narrative that says we are on our own in this world, and sometimes God shows up with a little blessing here and there?

Until the bride acknowledges and addresses her root issues of not trusting her Groom, she will continue to walk about in a foggy, hazy stupor brought on by worldly alternatives for faith. She will continue to treat the symptoms of her issues with numbing medications, with smooth speaking counselors, and with overcrowded calendars leaving no margin for the Spirit of God to move among her. Please do not hear us say there is no value in medication and professional counseling. We are confident God has, is and will continue to use these vehicles to deliver health and healing to people. Our express intent is to acknowledge and address the real problems along with the ultimate solution to those problems.

III. PTSD

> "Post-traumatic stress disorder (PTSD) is a mental health condition that's triggered by a terrifying event—either experiencing it or witnessing it. Symptoms may include flashbacks, nightmares and severe anxiety, as well as uncontrollable thoughts about the event."[18]

Now, let's face it, folks, the bride has tragically been knocked down a time or two. Oh, never by her perfect Groom. Only by her siblings— her brothers and sisters walking alongside

---

18   Mayo Clinic, "Post-traumatic stress disorder (PTSD)," overview, www. mayoclinic.org, retrieved October, 2018, https://www.mayoclinic.org/diseases-conditions/post-traumatic-stress-disorder/symptoms-causes/syc-20355967.

her on her faith journey with her groom. Sometimes it feels like the most emotionally dangerous place to step foot in is the local church— the body of Christ. People judge you there. People tell you what you're doing wrong there. People don't accept you as you are there. People only pretend to like you when you do what they want. People cease to like you when you don't do what they want. They have expectations, preferences, and traditions that you have to uphold to earn their love and acceptance.

Oddly enough, her siblings did not learn this behavior from their Father. You see, the Father loved them all, even when they were steeped in sin. The Father reached out and made a way to create fellowship with Him, even when their hearts were stone cold and turned away from Him. The Father gave when they didn't deserve it. The Father reached out when they pulled away. The Father loved when there was no love in return. The Father forgave even when He could have walked away. So why do the brothers and sisters of Christ treat each other with such contempt? Why do we inflict so many grievous wounds? Will it ever stop? Can we ever recover from our trauma?

Siblings fight when they want to be seen and heard. If a sibling feels threatened that maybe another sibling is stronger, better, or more gifted than they are, they might need to strike a blow to make themselves feel powerful and in control. A threat is a powerful thing. Adrenaline soars through our body, giving us incredible strength, speed, and call to action to protect! Protect! PROTECT! If our hearts feel threatened by forecasted loneliness, thoughts of being left out of the crowd, thoughts of being unnoticed and unheard by those we love, we will strike out. We can't beat our nature. Thankfully, Jesus went ahead and gave us a new one.

2 Corinthians 5:17 (NASB) Therefore if anyone is in Christ, he is a new creature; the old things passed away; behold, new things have come.

The redeeming work of Christ is not merely salvation; it is also the freeing of our captive souls. We bind ourselves up in need. We need approval and acceptance. We need the spotlight. We need to be number one. But Jesus comes, and He changes all of that. How? When the perfect Creator and God of the Universe shows up, you realize the spotlight has never belonged on you. The spotlight must shine only on Him. It is liberating when you realize you aren't the center of the universe because you also understand that seat has already been taken! Our old self, the one needing all power, control and let's face it, worship, is now replaced by the only One who is genuinely all-powerful, in control of everything and everyone, and the only perfect One worthy of worship.

Miraculously, our wounds heal when we stop looking to each other for our needs, and realize our Provider, Sustainer, and Friend has already granted to us all things that pertain to life and godliness, through the knowledge of Him who called us to His own glory and excellence (2 Peter 1:3). We must stop looking for our glory. We must stop looking to others to give us glory. We must stop attempting to control people and circumstances so that we are always the victor.

Friends, you cannot make it through a battle without wounds! So stop trying! Trust only in the Great Physician to heal you. Your friends can't do it for you. No amount of girl's nights, hunting trips, vacations or weekend getaways can do the work of your skilled Physician. You need the Creator, not the created, to do this amazing work on your heart and soul.

You'd best believe He made you that way for a purpose. He knows how quickly your wandering hearts stray. Thankfully, we have a built-in need for the fullness of Christ. We are incomplete without the great work of the Holy Spirit— alive and well in us. We need Him every hour. When each follower of Jesus seeks Him with their whole heart, He will be found, and their very hearts will be healed. They will be free from man-made shacks of tradition, and free to run in the freedom for which Christ set them free.

John 8:36 (ESV) So if the Son sets you free, you will be free indeed.

Galatians 5:1 (TPT) Let me be clear, the Anointed One has set us free—not partially, but completely and wonderfully free! We must always cherish this truth and stubbornly refuse to go back into the bondage of our past.

Can we be free from our spiritual PTSD? Count on it, friends. Free indeed. Remember, your purpose does not come from your passion or your paycheck. Passions are fickle, and paychecks are unreliable. Jesus is neither of those things. We tend to pursue things that stir in us passionate feelings and thoughts. We must not fall victim to the mindset that this is equal to God's calling on our lives and what it means to flesh out Matthew 16:24, Mark 8:34 and Luke 9:23.

> "If any man would come after me, let him deny himself." The disciple must say to himself the same words Peter said of Christ when he denied him: "I know not this man." Self-denial is never just a series of isolated acts of mortification or asceticism. It is not suicide, for there is an element of self-will even in that. To deny oneself is to be aware only of Christ and no more of self, to see only him who goes before and no more the road which is too hard for us. Once more, all that self denial can say is: "He leads the way, keep close to him." (Dietrich Bonhoeffer, The Cost of Discipleship)[19]

THE ENEMY

It is clear that we have an enemy that is behind so much of the darkness we encounter. It's this darkness that keeps us fumbling around and scared out of our minds. This is where the enemy does all his work. Let's talk about him and expose him a little bit before we wrap up this chapter. You'll see in mere moments how this radically affects people's identity.

ENOUGH...

The enemy's greatest lie is that what you have before you is not enough— God is not being completely honest and is withholding the REAL "best" for you. Remember, it was the original temptation that led to the actual sin, and is still

19   Bonhoeffer, Dietrich, "*The Cost of Discipleship*," Kindle location 1188 of 4738, TOUCHSTONE An Imprint of Simon & Schuster, Inc., 1995.

most effective today. It makes people leave jobs, churches, marriages, friendships, etc. See if any of these lies resonate with you:

- "Your job is not enough... doesn't God have more for me?"
- "Your church is not enough... I can find one bigger, better, tailored to my liking."
- "Your marriage isn't enough... could God have someone easier, better suited for me that I just missed along the way?"
- "Your friends are not enough... there are friends out there without so many issues, struggles— friends that will do more for me, treat me better, give me more."
- "Your house and possessions are not enough... didn't God call me to an abundant life? Wouldn't I have more if He wanted me to prosper? Isn't He withholding from me then? There is so much more material things to gain, why does He not want me to have them? Doesn't God care?"

The enemy considers it a victory when he can bring about discontent. We are discontent when we believe there is something more in the great beyond that surely God is withholding. So, we listen to the lies and begin to doubt the love and sovereignty of God and seek out our own personal destiny— become our personal rulers making our own paths to success and contentment.

Well meaning lies... (that we tell each other)

God will get you out of "here."

You will be prosperous in everything in every season.

God will deliver you from all pain and suffering (now).

"Life abundantly" is defined by you.

We leave the paths of what we truly have for the mirage of what might be out there— that if God truly loved us and had our best interest in mind, he would surely give to us. Remember, the enemy is the master deceiver, magician, slight of hand expert, etc. Here is his four-part goal and mission:

> First: To keep us from knowing, believing, and trusting God.
>
> Second: To keep us from growing in a personal love relationship with God.
>
> Third: To keep us from being in relationship with the people of God.
>
> Fourth: To keep us from telling others about the truth of God.

WHAT IS YOUR ID?

Identification: proof of who you are. The question every person wants an answer to is: "Who am I?" "What's my identity?" Based on what we believe about that will determine how we act and live out each day. God's Word offers an alternative to the crazy amount of methods we usually use to answer that question. Peter gives us great insight into who we are as Christians. In fact, the whole book seems to flow like water out of the well of this passage;

> *1 Peter 2:16 (NCV) Live as free people, but do not use your freedom as an excuse to do evil. Live as servants of God.*

Who wants to be free? Who wants to be free of the rat race of really discovering who they are? Listen, even the best of the best struggle with this, so don't be fooled or feel bad.

Do you ever wonder if we too often equate age with maturity? Of course, the body matures as we age, but it seems that too many people have fallen prey to the lie/assumption that spiritual maturity works the same way. If you have genuinely "tasted that the Lord is good," then you already have everything you need to want more— to want it all! But you have to stop limiting yourself as though you are on some spiritual diet. Be free! Today! There is a powerful message for us in 1 Peter 2:1-12 regarding your identity. In this text, you are given an eight-part perspective of your identity. Here they are in short (you can go back and read up on these any time):

I.   A Living Stone

II.   A Spiritual House

III.   A Chosen Race (people group)

IV.   A Royal Priesthood

V.   A Holy Nation

VI.   His Own Possession

VII. God's People

VIII. Sojourners

Let's spend just a few minutes on these last two.

God's People

God knew before the foundations of the earth were laid all who would call on His name for salvation. And He chose you, to have all eight of the above as part of who you are in Christ.

> *Romans 8:29-30 (ESV) For those whom he foreknew he also predestined to be conformed to the image of his Son, in order that he might be the firstborn among many brothers. And those whom he predestined he also called, and those whom he called he also justified, and those whom he justified he also glorified.*

Royal; set apart/holy. We represent the King of kings. We serve as priests. And we are called to be holy— not just individually, but as a people. A few is not enough. Majority is not enough.

1 Peter 1:15-16 (ESV) But as He who called you is holy, you also be holy in all your conduct, since it is written, "You shall be holy, for I am holy."

SOJOURNERS

This word is interesting in the Greek— it's likened to being aliens (not extraterrestrial), strangers, and foreigners. So why do we as Christians try so hard to fit in? No wonder so many struggle with an identity crisis. We're passing through. This is not our final stop. So we are free to stop living like this is it. Our final stop is incomparable to the here and now. We're here but for a moment. Use your time as a sojourner wisely, but this place/world is not our home. We will invest according to our belief concerning our identity.

> *Matthew 6:19-21 (ESV) Do not lay up for yourselves treasures on earth, where moth and rust destroy and where thieves break in and steal, but lay up for yourselves treasures in heaven, where neither moth nor rust destroys and where thieves do not break in and steal. For where your treasure is, there your heart will be also.*

What's keeping you from receiving your true identity in Christ? The rest of the world has offered you so many options to choose from. The enemy himself has a lot to say about you (and that started back in the garden with Adam and Eve). Your heart and head cannot live out sin and sanctity simultaneously. You indeed have to choose one. So how do you move successfully through this struggle known as "Identity Crisis?" It requires a healthy awareness and proper view of:

Your past

Your present

Your future

When we sin, we end up making poor choices and commit transgressions and iniquities (Iniquities- behavior that's crooked / Transgression- breaking trust). We live according to our fleshly desires and end up being slaves to our sin. Sin; *"Khata"* (Hebrew) *"Hamartia"* (Greek). Ultimately, it's not living in alignment with our identity as those created in God's image. It means we have missed the mark, failed, chosen incorrectly, taken the wrong path, etc. It means we are not living up to the standard of loving God and loving others (broken down in the ten commandments). By the way, this shows how amazing Jesus is. His life of no sin was given to cover our life of total sin, while we're still in sin (Romans 5:8).

See, you will live out what you think you are. You treat others the way you see them. However, your identity is not who you think you are, but who God says you are. Living out any other role other than your own is dangerous, debilitating and even destructive. Remember that you are a new creation and you are being made more and more into His likeness (2 Corinthians 5:16-21). And, don't be remiss and neglect what He is calling you into, a living hope (1 Peter 2:1-12). Something that can help you grab onto this truth is knowing that it's not just about your identity; it's about His.

Be where you are without living and preparing solely on where you're not, or where you think you should be. How about that for a mind twister? Ha! Live in a way that gives evidence of your walk with Jesus. Live in such a way that what you are doing right now is the most important thing you could be doing right now. Your body is a vehicle— a temple. Since the Spirit of God dwells in it, and you do too, then you are partners with Him in the same vehicle/body. It's like the Holy Spirit is the Captain, and you're the first mate of this vessel. He wants you to stay with Him at all times. Whenever you leave the bridge and run around your own ship, things start working improperly. And, the Holy Spirit is not just going to steer this thing while you're running around doing your own thing.

Paul's life completely changed after his encounter with Jesus. His purpose and point of being changed. He rarely knew where he was going to sleep, eat, etc. However, he knew who called him. He knew how to listen and follow. He knew how to give up all for the glory of God. Knowing his identity set him up for everything else. There is a powerful message here;

Ephesians 6:20 (TPT) Even though I am chained as a prisoner, I am His ambassador.

Wow! That one will stop you in your tracks. Here is a guy who was shipwrecked, beaten, naked, and in prison for a good part of his ministry. Why is this such a big deal? Because he did not allow his circumstances to determine his true calling and anointing. Who God says he was, and what God called him to do, could not be thwarted by even the most extreme situations and conditions— including being chained as a prisoner. But he wasn't a prisoner, was he? He was chained "as a prisoner." A very important distinction for our purposes of understanding true identity.

Remember, Paul even says this about himself;

Ephesians 1:1 (TPT) My name is Paul, and I was chosen by God to be an apostle of Jesus, the Messiah. His struggle was real, but his identity kept him from living as a victim.

CHRISTIANS DON'T STRUGGLE

This is a sentiment that has been expressed to so many Christians in countless settings and conversations. And, if it's true that Christians don't struggle, then how much more so for those who are called to be Christian leaders? This burden and lie has crushed many great Christian leaders.

It starts like this; all behavior is based on a belief. Behind every sin is a lie we're believing. One of the most important truths the Holy Spirit has to open our eyes to us is that Christians do in fact struggle. You talk about a massive reframe! Once your eyes are opened to God's heart towards those who were not perfect in Scripture, you begin to find your hearts drawn closer to them. You'll notice Him speaking more and more about valleys, darkness, hard times, persecution, failures, etc. Your heart and eyes will finally see on a deeper more practical level how He was, and remains, God over all of those times, places, and experiences.

HE IS THE GOD OF YOUR VALLEYS:

He causes us to go through some of our valleys

He allows us to go through all of our valleys

He can use each of our valleys for our good

HE WILL USE THEM TO:

Build Character

- Remembering the past
- Reading the Word
- Relying on fellow believers (bear one another's burdens)

Accomplish His Purpose

- He will do this not just in your life, but in the lives of others

Teach Us To Rely On Him

- Even when things seem they are at their worst, He is sufficient

There is such liberty and life-giving truth in knowing that it's reasonable to struggle. And how much more so that God does some of His greatest work during those times. This not only changes your perspective about struggle but changes your reaction to it, even while you are still in it. It also changes the way you see yourself and others. It certainly makes more sense when we read truths from the Bible like this one:

1 Corinthians 1:26-31 (NLT) 26 Remember, dear brothers and sisters, that few of you were wise in the world's eyes or powerful or wealthy when God called you. 27 Instead, God chose things the world considers foolish in order to shame those who think they are wise. And he chose things that are powerless to shame those who are powerful. 28 God chose things despised by the world, things counted as nothing at all, and used them to bring to nothing what the world considers important. 29 As a result, no one can ever boast in the presence of God. 30 God has united you with Christ Jesus. For our benefit God made him to be wisdom itself. Christ made us right with God; he made us pure and holy, and he freed us from sin. 31 Therefore, as the Scriptures say, "If you want to boast, boast only about the Lord."

What happens when Christians believe they don't struggle? We start believing that something is wrong— is it, people? God? The place where we are? We have to "find" it and label it. We have a constant sense of "if only something external would change," or "what if I had more faith, then I would not be struggling, or coming up short." Maybe if we try hard enough, or have more faith, or if we strive harder to be more like those who are not struggling, then perhaps, just maybe, we would not be struggling like we are. Have you ever felt like this before? You're not alone. The comparison and blame games aren't new. They can be traced back even to the first two people on earth.

ADAM/EVE (RE: LIES ABOUT GOD):

We love to point fingers and pass on the fault to others. Blame it on someone or something. Sometimes we even find ourselves indirectly blaming God through someone else or some other circumstance. It's easy to believe what God gives us is not truly sufficient. God is withholding better things from us. God must not have our best interest in mind. Maybe God's commands are optional and up for our interpretation. Now it's easy to start doubting God and disobedience starts looking beneficial to us— you know, since He is withholding the best from us. If this sounds familiar (and be honest), then it's time to take inventory and look just how far back the roots of these lies you have believed go.

If we believe that God is withholding from us, then we will find ourselves believing and living in a false narrative (an all too common one at that). Then we move into taking our future in our own hands, then lying to protect ourselves. This leads to a dangerous place as a Christian where we think failure is not an option. We believe we can live like those actively involved in sin and not be affected. What a lie!

The final destination in this journey of believing and living a lie looks much like a man we all know very well, David (King David from the book of Samuel in the Old Testament). It's so easy to end up pursuing anything we desire. Pursuing sin will have no consequence to those around us. Hurting others to conceal our sin is acceptable. Our sin isn't known to others. Our sin will not come to light. Well, if you have spent any time in the Old Testament, you know quite well just how wrong and harmful this mindset is.

Most of us have been guilty of getting comfortable with hearing stories without knowing their context and internalizing their real intent. Maybe you have heard about how we once were lost, and now we're found, and perhaps that's your only understanding of redemption. If so, did you know there's more to it than that?

Redemption is the act of buying something back. Christ repurchased us from eternal separation from the Father at the cost of His own life. But redemption doesn't have to stop there. There are always areas in our lives that we can open up to His redemptive work, a continual buying back, to release us from whatever is holding us back in our walk with Him (this is part of sanctification). Please allow us to use this passage once again so it might settle deep and fast in our hearts and heads. Check it out from The Message;

> *Galatians 5:1 (MSG) Christ has set us free to live a free life. So take your stand! Never again let anyone put a harness of slavery on you.*

So there's a churchy sounding word we throw around called idolatry. The root of the word is Idol. So what's an idol? Anything that you exalt or look up to more than Jesus. Anything you seek first— anything that is more treasured and precious to you than Christ is more than likely a dangerous idol in your life. In Old Testament history, idols were typically statues of wood or stone, formed by craftsman into the likeness of a person or animal or a combo of both. People believed those statues then had powers to save— to create life, to bring rain, to heal, etc.

Before you take inventory and think you're off the hook, let's fast forward to today. Idols today are anything or anyone that consumes your heart and mind more than Jesus. I once heard a pastor ask the question, "Where do you derive your greatest security? That, is your God." Pretty simple. And yet not.

While many never believe a statue could help them find their way in life, often they think other human beings can. They buy into lies that cause them to believe a particular person or group of people is all they need to be truly happy. If they are down, they will often turn to a friend before turning to the Lord. They will rely on others to change their mood, make them feel better, or help them feel accepted. People can so quickly become idols. And it is always costly. Sure, they still love God, but He probably doesn't consume their waking hours like thoughts of, and conversations with friends or family do.

Please know one thing about our Father. Scripture tells us He detests idols. He despises them because He loves us. He knows we're at our best when we are consumed with Him (His love and His Word) and when He is at the center of our reality. So, what choice does a loving Father have but to make sure that which is harmful to His children is taken away? Yes, in our lifetime God has seen fit more than once to remove us from the idols in our lives, and it is usually dreadfully painful. But you know what? We're always better for it on the other side. We're wiser. We're more watchful. We strive to lean into Him rather than lean into others when the going gets rough. He reminds us there is no person on earth with the power to save. That work is already done and finished for us on the cross.

So whether your idol (that thing that consumes you, that person, place or something that you treasure and trust) is your job, your car, your house, your shoes, your friends or your spouse, would you join us in stumbling forward into eternity? Ask the Lord if there is anything or anyone that might be taking His rightful place in your life? Then join us in celebrating our true freedom found at the foot of the cross, where we can lay every burden and idol, past and present, down at the feet of Jesus. Come with us, friends! Freedom is waiting!

GETTING A LITTLE MORE PERSONAL

What things, events, beliefs or people do you remember having profound effects in and on your life and faith development? This is a big question, so take your time allowing the Holy Spirit to reveal these things to you. You can trust Him.

1 Peter 5:7 tells us that we are to cast all our burdens on Jesus because He cares for us. And quite frankly, He is the only One that can do anything about them. So, what are those anxieties that are keeping you from walking in the freedom that you have been set free to experience? Will you trust Him enough to give those to Him? You may have to do this multiple times a day for many days— but the key is to do it! Think about this powerful truth regarding your new identity in Christ;

> *Revelation 12:11 (CEV) Our people defeated Satan because of the blood of the Lamb and the message of God. They were willing to give up their lives.*

You see, it's the blood of the Lamb that gives credibility and power to the testimony we give about the message of God in Christ. It's the power of the Holy Spirit that works powerfully in and through you. So, here's the truth to consider and work through— will you receive by faith the finished work of Christ in your life? Will you allow God to use you as His witnesses regardless of whether you think you are qualified? This reframe will radically alter your self-image and open up exponentially more opportunities than you ever thought possible!

CHAPTER 8

PRAYER

MORE THAN WORDS.

AND NOW, LET US PRAY!

Prayer is interesting. We have heard all kinds of explanations on prayer. Most of them (in their best efforts) leaving us with more confusion, guilt and a general sense of failure and frustration. A significant part of this is because most people believe it and practice based on the outcome of prayer (receiving what they asked for in the manner in which they asked for it).

When God answers your prayers the way you asked, then to God be the glory. But happens when He doesn't? Are we still compelled to love and obey Him? People will often take up the issue with God's decision to act in accordance with their specific requests (presuming they know best).

Maybe the more significant underlying issue is not what we are asking for, but why we ask. If everything is to bring

God glory, and intimacy with the Father is the driving force for asking anything of Him, then it would stand to reason that if we walk in sweet fellowship with Him that we are more concerned with His will than our own. When we ask in His name and give Him the room to answer correctly, we will always be thankful and full of rejoicing, no matter the outcome.

We can do this because we will believe that His answer to us is what we want, even if we are unable to understand or articulate it that way. We want what is best for us, right? If so, we can rest assured that however He responds is fulfilling that greater request (the ask behind the ask).

God's goodness is not confined or subject to the outcome of a particular prayer. No matter how earnest or how many people prayed for that request. Otherwise, we'd feel slighted that God did not move or respond in the way we inadvertently tried manipulating Him into. It is unwise to present God a small list of multiple choice ways He can answer. He refuses to stay in line with our personal theology and give support to our own doctrines and disciplines pertaining to His Word. We can assure you that you will in no way experience the fullness and favor of God with this mindset.

Even as we write this book, prayer has been a major ongoing and morphing reframe for us. The elementary principle that you might find obvious at first is that prayer is a two-way street and requires: coming and going, listening and talking, as well as giving and receiving. We have walked alongside some of the most excellent lovers of Jesus, and still, so many of them have been perplexed by prayer. Consequently, many of us have heard and used passages in the Bible like this;

Romans 8:26 (ESV) Likewise the Spirit helps us in our weakness. For we do not know what to pray for as we ought, but the Spirit Himself intercedes for us with groanings too deep for words.

We thank the Holy Spirit for His role in understanding our conversations, crazy sentences and thoughts, feelings and emotions and yes, even moans and groans that we have no other way to express. However, our problem regarding prayer is not the lack of clarity in our words, or the ability to articulate with eloquence. Isaiah gives us great insight into the issues that God took up with His people regarding prayer.

Issue of Apathy (Isaiah 1:1-9)

Issue of Authenticity (Isaiah 1:10-15)

Issue of Action (Isaiah 1:16-20)

These are three issues God had with His people. How do you see these issues played out in your life? How about in your church? Are your prayers powerful or powerless? Do you see the Holy Spirit moving in and through your life, family and church because of prayer?

Power through praying together has everything to do with what you're asking for and why. When God's people have unity in the things that Christ Himself had with His Father, we know we're on track to receive power in those prayers.

Three great questions to ask yourselves even now:

First: What am I asking for?

Second: Why am I asking for it?

Third: What am I willing to do to be a part of the answer?

For God, part of the point in being unified in prayer is us coming together as His family. How does praying together bring us together? How does it affect who we are as individuals, and as a church body? He wants that time personally with Him as well as us along with other believers. That's not all. He wants us to believe Him. He wants us to pray His promises. This is why we find such great hope and comfort in Scripture like the following;

2 Corinthians 1:20 (NLT) For all of God's promises have been fulfilled in Christ with a resounding "Yes!" And through Christ, our "Amen" (which means "Yes") ascends to God for His glory.

"It is impossible to develop powerful Biblical prayer without joining your prayers to the promises of God."[20]

Part of your reframe when it comes to prayer will be learning simple strategies that are personal, practical and relevant to who and where you are.

Matthew 6:5-13 is action-packed and begins with this statement, "When you pray." This is saturated with the assumption that, as a committed follower of Jesus, you will pray. We would argue that the issue is not if people pray (communication), but who they are praying to. What are people doing when they pray? What are they expecting when they pray? Etc. Believers, we need to be intentional when we pray. Mind, mouth, and body communicates with God. Even our very being is continuously communicating.

Here is what we know about prayer from this model given us by Jesus in that same passage of Scripture. There is first of all intimacy in prayer (Matthew 6:6a). Remember who you are talking to. It's personal, and it's to a person(s)— the Father, Son, Holy Spirit. A pastor-friend of ours, Destined Wright from Brentwood Neighborhood Church, said it very short and sweet, "Prayer is dependency." It's perfect! When we are completely dependent on Him, prayer comes alive! It radically changes our lives from the inside out. Notice the order there- from the inside first, then the outward manifestation of the answered prayers.

In that same sermon from Pastor Destined, he pointed out that the disciples must have had some understanding of this. Maybe this is why they asked in Luke 11:1 for Jesus to teach them to pray. They didn't ask Him to teach them to heal or do miracles. They would have known by now that all the cool stuff (miracles, signs, and wonders) came out of prayer— that's where the power source was found and released. This is what makes these next two passages come alive.

John 15:7 (TPT) But if you live in life-union with Me and if My words live powerfully within you —then you can ask whatever you desire and it will be done.

20   Frizzell, Dr. Gregory, "How To Develop A Powerful Prayer Life," Master Design, First Edition edition, August 31, 2000.

Psalm 145:18-19 (ESV) The Lord is near to all who call on Him, to all who call on Him in truth. He fulfills the desire of those who fear Him; He also hears their cry and saves them.

James Dwyer has much to say about flourishing prayer in his book, *"Why Is Prayer So Hard?"* Here is an excerpt from that book:

> "A flourishing prayer life comes not out of dedication to rules and regulations—although structure may help—but from the overflow of a heart totally and fully in love with God. Human relationships thrive when both parties communicate with each other as motivated by love, and prayer requires the same foundation. If we are not overflowing with God's love, our prayer lives will reflect that."21

We said that there was first intimacy in prayer. We also see that there is confidence in prayer according to Matthew 6:6b. This is a cornerstone truth to the effectiveness of your prayer life. Out of this intimate communion with the Father, Son, and Holy Spirit comes confidence in whatever you are asking because you are praying according to God's will. This, of course, assumes that you walk with God and walk according to His Word. That changes your will to His will. That's why asking anything in His name is given (in one way or another).

Mark 11:24 (ESV) Therefore I tell you, whatever you ask in prayer, believe that you have received it, and it will be yours.

1 John 5:14-15 (TPT) Since we have this confidence, we can also have great boldness before Him, for if we present any request agreeable to His will, He will hear us. And if we know that He hears us in whatever we ask, we also know that we have obtained the requests we ask of Him.

---

21   Dwyer, James, *"Why Is Prayer So Hard?,"* Article, www. relevantmagazine.com, January, 2013, retrieved October, 2015, https:// relevantmagazine.com/god/practical-faith/why-prayer-so-hard.

Praying with authenticity and confidence to God means very little apart from intimacy with Him (Matthew 6:7-8). Prayer is not about being pious or pithy. Prayer is about Kingdom perspective that comes from a personal relationship. Paul told the church in Romans 12 to make sure their love was genuine. People have said, "fake it till you make it." That may be applicable for many things, but not prayer. God knows your heart because you have the Holy Spirit that has taken up residence in you. So, there will be no faking it. Trust us; we have tried. Ha! Jesus even told His disciples to be earnest in their prayer because it would have a significant effect on the Kingdom.

Adoration in prayer is so essential, and honestly a delight (Matthew 6:9). How incredible it is to know God as your Father, and to know where He reigns and resides. You are adoring Him as He is— Holy. So we revere Him in the highest regard. Praise and worship the Lord. We desire our prayers to be like a fragrant incense offered freely in worship (Psalm 141:2). Praying the 23rd Psalm is also a powerful way to align yourself with who He is (your Shepherd), what He does (leads, provides and comforts you), and what the benefits and promises are for those who belong to Him.

There is also surrender in Prayer (Matthew 6:10). This requires action on our part. We have to surrender. He won't make us surrender because it's an act of love and submission based on love and trust. Surrendering in prayer is believing confidently in Him to the point of action and praying with hands and feet, not just mind and mouth. It's being Kingdom-minded and caring genuinely about His purpose and His plan is made real here on earth. It's praying at a depth where the emphasis is not you, or about you directly. Try that.

1 Timothy 2:1-4 (TPT) Most of all, I'm writing to encourage you to pray with gratitude to God. Pray for all men with all forms of prayers and requests as you intercede with intense passion. 2 And pray for every political leader and representative, so that we would be able to live tranquil, undisturbed lives, as we worship the awe-inspiring God with pure hearts. 3 It is pleasing to our Savior-God to pray for them. 4 He longs for everyone to embrace his life and return to the full knowledge of the truth.

Dependency in Prayer for God's provisions is essential for a full and productive life (Matthew 6:11). We are trusting God for life's needs. For many, this is part of a major reframe seems impossible. Don't be discouraged. Remember, this is only possible when Christ rules in and through you. Even though we must pray without the emphasis being on us, there is still an intimacy component here that shows He cares for us to the degree that we can bring Him those things that in the bigger picture may seem trivial.

> "Those two things— glorifying God and enjoying God— do not always coincide in this life, but in the end they must be the same thing. We may pray for the coming of God's kingdom, but if we don't enjoy God supremely with all our being, we are not truly honoring him as Lord. Prayer is both awe and intimacy, struggle and reality. These will not happen every time we pray, but each should be a major component of our prayer over the course of our lives."[22]

Another area of difficulty in regards to prayer is forgiveness (Matthew 6:12). There is a deep stirring within us when we are in constant intimacy with the Father. The Holy Spirit shows where we are not in oneness with Christ— where we are missing the mark. This is why there has to be forgiveness. For that to happen, there has to be confession and repentance on our part.

Knowing your propensity for sin and God's incredible grace and mercy should make it more common for us to forgive others. However, it seems like we still want to be forgiven more than we want to forgive. Just know this (in case you were wondering), your life is never better if you choose not to forgive. It will eat you up inside and out. Forgiveness from God sets you free. Forgiving others is not only the

22   Keller, Timothy, *"Experiencing Awe And Intimacy With God,"* Kindle Location 121 of 4830, A Penguin Random House Company, 2014.

natural reaction of one that has been forgiven but will also allow you to live and operate in that freedom (not to mention being a catalyst for others to operate in forgiveness as well). The Psalmist said if he had closed his eyes to his sin, God would have closed His ears to the Psalmist's prayer (Psalm 66:18).

> "We must develop and maintain the capacity to forgive. He who is devoid of the power to forgive is devoid of the power to love. There is some good in the worst of us and some evil in the best of us. When we discover this, we are less prone to hate our enemies." -Martin Luther King, Jr.[23]

Using Matthew's account of what Jesus instructed regarding prayer, there is direction offered us through prayer that will save our lives (Matthew 6:13). This direction will always lead us away from temptation and deliver us from the snares of evil. What is the opposite of being led into temptation? If He is leading us not into temptation, then He is leading us somewhere else. Psalm 34:17 says He leads us into deliverance. Another part of His leading is His protection. Psalm 91:1 says you will abide in the shadow of the Almighty when you dwell in Him.

The point is this, prayer is communion with God and starts with dependency on Him. It is relational before it is anything else. It is to change us and conform us more into the image of Christ. It is where we draw our power through the work of the Holy Spirit. It is where we do our most significant work in battle. Our primary purpose for asking anything of Him is not for the outcome of our request, but out of obedience—believing He has His best and your good in His response.

23 King, Martin Luther, Jr., Quotes. (n.d.). BrainyQuote.com, retrieved August 3, 2019, https://www.brainyquote.com/quotes/martin_luther_king_jr_143179.

A POWERFUL PRAYER LIFE!

Here are some questions that would be good for you to wrestle through. Don't be afraid to do this with others as well.

Why are prayer and the Bible inseparable?
- What are the dangers of praying without Scripture being our basis for those prayers?
- What are you hearing in your life right now because of your time in the Word?
- How can we pray together for each other and for our church using what God is speaking to us through His Word?

More great passages on prayer for your own personal study and encouragement.

Ephesians 6:18, Colossians 4:2, 1 Thessalonians 5:17, James 4:3, 5:13-16, Jeremiah 29:12, Matthew 9:35-38

Waiting on the Lord is difficult in prayer. How do you manage your patience (or lack thereof) when you are praying, and waiting? There is a generous promise for you when you take on the mindset of Isaiah's words;

Isaiah 40:31 (ESV) But they who wait for the Lord shall renew their strength; they shall mount up with wings like eagles; they shall run and not be weary; they shall walk and not faint.

SECTION 3

THE CHURCH REFRAMED

CHAPTER 9

THE CHURCH - PART 1

"THE MISSION"

Can you recite from memory your church's mission statement? Do you have a mission statement for your own life? Here's an interesting thing to do, Google "church mission statements" and see the endless list before you. Mission statements are not wrong in and of themselves. However, the ones that are based in Scripture tend to all sound the same, just worded differently. Jesus gave a commissioning statement to His disciples, the apostles in Matthew 28. This was their mission.

Shortly after the inception of the local church in the New Testament, individuals and churches began taking what Jesus said and did and tailoring them to who they were and wanted to be. A great question to ask yourself when you think about a mission and mission statement— Does my mission statement and the church's mission statement ever meet? Or do they collide?

It may be easier to start like this— you, me, and all the

other redeemed are the very ones that make up the church. Can you imagine Jesus giving each of His followers specific missions? That would be crazy and chaotic. That's why the mission of the church and the mission for your life go hand in hand. That should make sense to us since we know the church is made up of people and not property. We see this missional mindset described in Matthew 28:16-20.

PERSONALLY (IN THE CHURCH)

When Jesus charged His disciples with the responsibility to go, His charge was to fulfill the mission. In similar ways, this was the mission Jesus was given by His Father, to redeem man and restore them into a right relationship with Himself. Since the goal of a successful disciple-maker is to produce other disciple-makers, the emphasis is not just on the one person you reach (although the one is infinitely important to Jesus). It's making sure those individuals you are investing in not only know how to disciple but encouraging them to do it as well. This process and mindset of making disciple-makers is an excellent indicator of being a healthy disciple yourself.

Another important perspective regarding our mission is establishing and remembering who we are following, and who we are discipling others to follow (Christ, and not ourselves). This is not a mission we can put on the shoulders of those who are getting paid to lead and serve in our local churches and ministries. This is the responsibility (as well as joy and honor) of every child of God. We are to be ready if anyone asks us why we have this hope (1 Peter 3:15). We are to make a conscious effort to share the gospel with anyone who will listen (Mark 16:15). Our mission is to speak joyfully and boldly without shame.

The power of God is released to anyone who would receive salvation (Romans 1:16). This is not just a New Testament consideration or command. Even God expected His people to be His witnesses in all the world (Isaiah 43:10). So these are our responsibilities as individuals. Let's see what it looks like when we do it together.

TOGETHER (AS THE CHURCH)

We can always do more together (in Jesus' name) than we can alone. Praise God for the individual roles and responsibilities He has given us. The great thing is, they're best used and fulfilled in us and through us when we are in partnership with other followers of Christ. Together, we have a mission to accomplish. A major reframe might start with a good healthy look at what that mission is not.

THE MISSION OF THE CHURCH IS NOT:

Denominational Dynasties

Although grateful for the benefits that we received from being in denominational churches, the mission of the church is not tailored to specific denominations. Denominations have merit and value when they operate out of a spirit of humility, cooperation, and accountability. Many have said it before, but it still bears great truth; when people work out of a denominational and territorial mindset, they are relegated to gathering when there is agreement but segregating when there is disagreement.

Megachurch Models

Large churches are not inherently wrong, but they are also not the standard. The people leading the major movements are not the boilerplate paradigm for the church as a whole. Growing big enough to have more satellite churches than actual satellites in the sky is certainly not the missional model given by Jesus (or any other writer in the Scriptures). Remember, big is not bad. How you get there, why you are there, what you do there— these are some of the considerations to help determine whether they are healthy or not.

Small-Minded Assemblies

Just like being big is not the standard, being intentionally small isn't either. There are plenty of churches that have the mentality that staying small is the mission and mindset for real success. One major problem with this mindset is that the greater good is lost in self-preservation. It acts as a way to keep the "bad people" out to protect what remains of the "good people" inside. Often, the groups that like to meet in homes, will have to wrestle with how to function in the fullness intended by God due to the absence of the full range of gifts given by the Holy Spirit for His church. The same considerations for the large church are equally applicable here in the small churches.

THE MISSION OF THE CHURCH IS:

It may be helpful to think of the mission of the church in alliteration form. As you probably know, preachers and teachers love alliterations. It's useful in remembering major concepts and truths. So, here's one that might make it easier in remembering the mission of the church (and our responsibilities to that mission). The Mission Of The Church is - **R.E.A.L**

Relational

The mission of the church is relational. This is foundational. This is the make or break when it comes to the true effectiveness in accomplishing the mission given us by Jesus Himself.

Evangelistic

The church has a tremendous responsibility of bringing the good news to the world. Unfortunately, many churches don't make it into their own neighbor's property lines in reaching the wayward, misled and dying with the good new of Jesus (John 14:6).

Apostolic

The mission of the church is an apostolic mission ("sent ones"). We're not talking bout a particular movement, denomination or affiliation. The church from the very beginning was an apostolic one, and is still such today. Since we know the church is not a building, a piece of property, an individual's idea or dream, then it goes without saying the the mission of the church is also none of those things (although often times they are used as effective tools and vehicles).

Long-term

One critical reframe for all of us is learning to start with the end in mind. The mission is a long-term one. It's not a sprint, as many throughout the generations have stated. It's a marathon. It will not be completed until Jesus returns. This truth is critical in determining the length and quality of life for any church.

> "The word mission comes from the Latin words mitto (to send) and missio (sending). So mission implies that someone has sent something to accomplish a task. In other words, God has sent the church to accomplish a task."[24]

What is the correct understanding of our mission? Are we engaged with that mission (as we understand it defined)? What are the actual imperatives and mandates associated with this mission (and what practically is our part)? "Mission" in the context of Scripture is often exercised much differently today. Going back to what Jesus told His apostles— mission is about completing an investment and/or assignment. People are the assignment and investment. Discipleship is not a peripheral ideology or suggested discipline, but the core of the Christian's purpose and mission.

Let's go back to Matthew 28:16-20 and look at it a little closer.

> *Matthew 28:16-20 (TPT) 16 Meanwhile, the eleven disciples heard the wonderful news from the women and left for Galilee, to the mountain where Jesus had arranged to meet them. 17 The moment they saw him, they worshiped him, but some still had lingering doubts. 18 Then Jesus came close to them and said, "All the*

24   Hilgemann, Brandon, "*What Is The Mission Of The Church?*," www.propreacher.com, May, 2018, retrieved June, 2018, https://www.propreacher.com/what-is-the-mission-of-the-church/.

authority of the universe has been given to me. 19 Now go in my authority and make disciples of all nations, baptizing them in the name of the Father, the Son, and the Holy Spirit. 20 And teach them to faithfully follow all that I have commanded you. And never forget that I am with you every day, even to the completion of this age."

Matthew starts off this portion of his writings by acknowledging three things (which are common to us even today):

1st- Jesus called them together in one place to hear from Him (which was a miracle in and of itself)

2nd- The believers/followers worshipped (natural response)

3rd- Some doubted— not everyone will believe right away at face value or at first sight (Thomas)

He called them there to give them some of the most important instruction they would ever receive. He had one mission for them. All other teachings would fall under the umbrella of this one. Maybe that's why Jesus gathered them together and started with the power statement of the day, "All authority in heaven and on earth has been given to Me." Based on that truth, His next statements are couched in the word, "Therefore." You must have something pretty important to say when you lead off with that kind of verbiage.

I. GO (NEAR AND FAR INTO THE WORLD)

The assumption is that you are already doing that... (as you go). Start where you are, then keep going further out. Sure, some will be called out further in geography and sacrifice than others. However, the obedience to the command is the same.

Acts 1:8 (ESV) But you will receive power when the Holy Spirit has come upon you, and you will be my witnesses in Jerusalem and in all Judea and Samaria, and to the end of the earth.

II. MAKE DISCIPLES (DISCIPLE-MAKING DISCIPLES)

This Starts with sharing your story and His story (many Christians call this "witnessing"). You have the honor and privilege of sharing yours, and His, amazing story of grace. Remember, this requires living in missional community (highly relational) where you actively participate in transparency, humility, surrender and a general sense of living life with others. For further study, Titus 2 gives more instruction as to how we invest in each other using sound doctrine, older teaching the younger, etc.

Part of healthy disciple-making includes this simple but often avoided command to obey in all things. One of the unfortunate areas so many Christians have not been obedient in is baptism. It's part of the mission. It's not just seeing people come to know Christ, but as it is possible, being baptized in the wonderful name of the Father, Son, and Holy Spirit. This simple act of obedience is often the catalyst that springs Christians into an entirely different realm of purpose and usefulness in His Kingdom work.

III. TEACH DISCIPLES (WHATEVER JESUS TAUGHT THEM)

Part of our responsibility in this mission is to teach others the sound teachings we have been taught. Another reframe here—the emphasis is not what others have explained, but what the Holy Spirit has shown you from God's Word (regardless of who delivered it or how it came to you). Please do not miss this. There are a lot of smart people out there with an incredible education, powerful insights, and convincing arguments. Hey, many of them are spot on (as much as any one human can be). However, none of them is your primary source for insight, revelation, understanding or power to respond to them. This role has been reserved for the Holy Spirit who serves as the primary teacher to those who will study the Scriptures and allow Him to work it out in and through them.

Knowing, believing and living out God's Word is not an

option. Teaching others (whether it's your spiritual gift or not) God's Word is also not an option. Not everyone should be quick to call themselves a teacher. We're not speaking of the role and gift of a teacher here. We're talking about the investment that we are to make in other's lives regarding the truths of God's Word that we have learned and live. Teach them to observe all that Jesus has commanded them (to listen, learn and obey). This requires more than a stop-and-go relationship and investment.

Jesus models true discipleship. His mission and method were to attach Himself to willing believers and make them extensions of Himself. True discipleship is a mission with a dual relationship of reaching and teaching. It's essential for faith development to know the who, what, where, when, how and why of the mission. These are all things that the Holy Spirit teaches us when we take the time to invest in each other. Can you see why the mission matters so much?!

Hardships, hurdles, and hangups are to be expected in our lives as we walk in fellowship with one another (as the church). This is why it's so essential for us not to forget passages like Romans 5:3-5. Paul tells the church we can have confidence even in the hard times. These are the moments that develop in us patience, endurance, character, and even hope. He also writes to the Corinthian church to remind them that although their troubles may seem monumental, they are quite small in comparison to what they will gain in eternity and for eternity (2 Corinthians 4:17)! Thank God that message is still real and relevant for us today.

One great thing we've discovered is, when individuals are more concerned about investing in people with the gospel than investing in the politics of self-promotion, God can accomplish a more significant work through those people. This reframe would in return completely change the face of the modern day Evangelical/Protestant/Christian church as we know it.

The mission still matters today. "Mission(s)" is not just a ministry, occupation, program in the church, series of trips taken overseas— it's a life we are all called to in one way or another. There is a general calling with most gifts as well as offices for specific purposes, places, and seasons. Living on mission matters because THE mission matters. Therefore, our response to the roles and responsibilities God has placed on each of us in His church matters.

> **Mission Matters**: there are two different ways to use this (both are right).

> Mission matters— it is a fact and way of life.

> Mission matters— the principles, actions and ways of life we're all called to live by.

> Two reasons we have not been able to reach the community at large:

> Personal obedience - great commandment and commission

> Corporate obedience - learning, loving, and investing in our current culture and context while investing in all generations for the sake of reaching all generations.

In Matthew 10, Jesus called the twelve apostles individually out of their former vocations. He gave them authority over the spiritual realm and authority to heal every sickness and affliction. He specifically called the twelve to the lost sheep of Israel. This was their mission.

HIS INSTRUCTIONS:

Jesus instructed them not to go to the Gentiles. Apostles had a specific call to the Israelites. They would have already been under a deeply rooted religious structure. He instructed them not to focus on acquiring wealth or possessions, but said they would be provided for. He instructed them to find and align themselves with those who are worthy in each town, and to stay with them. He tells them to let their peace fall on the house of the worthy, and that if it is found not to be worthy, let the peace return to back to them. They were told if anyone would not receive or listen to their words in those towns, they were to shake the dust off their feet and leave.

HIS PROMISES:

He promises they are being sent as sheep (followers who know the masters voice) among wolves. The religious structure devours truth bearers. Wisdom will be needed.

He promises the wolves will flog them in the synagogue— their place of religious structure. Men will deliver them over to the governmental courts and involve those outside their religious system to persecute them.

Jesus promises the apostles they will be hated because of Him, stating when they are persecuted in one town, flee to the next. He also states they will not even be able to make it through all the towns before the end of the age— meaning, persecution would be found wherever they would go for as long as they would go.

HIS REMINDERS:

Jesus reminds the apostles they are seen and greatly valued by their Father.

Jesus reminds them His work is not about bringing peace to this world, but a sword. His sword will bring division, even among households. And, whoever does not take up their cross is not worthy to follow Him.

Jesus reminds them that whoever receives them receives Jesus. And whoever rejects them is actually rejecting Jesus. They were not to be anxious about what to say in front of the courts, for it will not be them speaking, but the Spirit of their Heavenly Father.

In the midst of promises of hate and persecution from those

who claim to be religious, Jesus ultimately instructs them not to panic under the pressure. He reminds them everything hidden will be revealed in time. Whatever message the apostles were given in the dark was to be spoken in the light and without fear. Whatever whisper they heard from the Spirit was to be proclaimed boldly from the rooftops.

MISSION ACCOMPLISHED!

The mission of the church has not changed. The motivation behind the mission has not changed. Therefore, we have been given all we need in order to be able to say one day, "Mission Accomplished!" Like the man in the parable Jesus taught about, we want to hear our Master's approval and affirmation;

> *Matthew 25:23 (ESV) Well done, good and faithful servant. You have been faithful over a little; I will set you over much. Enter into the joy of your master.*

The Warning: If we do not get this reframe correct, it causes us to get off track in every other area of the church (her message, missionaries, and methods). We must get the mission right!

What do you believe about the mission of the church? Do you believe it is still relevant to our culture today? To the world? How so?

What role do you sense God has for you in this mission? What keeps you from jumping in head first?

Be encouraged, just as you are imperfect, so is the church. Most churches out there are not looking for perfect people. They are looking for those who are willing to walk together in submission to the Spirit of God as they accomplish the work set before them by Jesus as expressed in His Word. Give it a shot. For some of you, give it another chance! It's the only way we're going to be able to say in our last words, "Mission Accomplished!"

CHAPTER 10

THE CHURCH - PART 2

"THE MESSAGE"

GOOD NEWS!

What's the Good News? The Good News is The Gospel. And, The Gospel is The Message.

> *Mark 1:15 (TPT) His message was this: "At last the fulfillment of the age has come! It is time for the realm of God's kingdom to be experienced in its fullness! Turn your lives back to God and put your trust in the hope-filled gospel!"*

O yeah, and The Message is The Way, The Truth, and The Life (John 14:6). All of this is wrapped up into a person, and His name is Jesus. It's all about Jesus. For man, it's always been about Jesus. Being in right relationship isn't possible without

Jesus. Because of Jesus and the completed work on the cross, we can now have eternal life with the Father! That's the Good News. That's The Gospel. That's The Message!

The message is one of freedom. There is a way that people can escape not only the throes of eternal hell and separation from God, but also a way into an intimate relationship with the Heavenly Father, by salvation through the Savior Jesus Christ, by the powerful work of the Holy Spirit. The message is one of hope. Salvation. Healing. This message is for every person at every station in life. Lost. Saved. And, although the Spirit of God has the responsibility to genuinely lead people to Jesus and respond to the message of salvation, we walk in partnership and surrender to the Holy Spirit— we are a blessed people to be a part of this process.

THE CATCH AND THE CAUTION:

There is a prophetic warning that we are living out as we write.

> 2 Timothy 4:3-4 (NLV) 3 The time will come when people will not listen to the truth. They will look for teachers who will tell them only what they want to hear. 4 They will not listen to the truth. Instead, they will listen to stories made up by men.

It seems this message has been made real and current. Before we jump any furthering into the message, it is imperative that we wake up and pay attention to the reality of this catch and caution. We are indeed living in a day and age where people who identify themselves as Bible-believing are anything but. Many have sadly become numb to the message of God and are chasing after the messages of men. This has an unfortunate end.

> Proverbs 14:12 (TPT) You can rationalize it all you want and justify the path of error you have chosen, but you'll find out in the end that you took the road to destruction.

Paul provided us with a great perspective through so many of his messages. His messages were (for the most part) simple. He wrote to churches as well as individuals. Amid these letters of correction, instruction, and encouragement, never lose sight of his primary message. The main thrust of his preaching and teaching is said best here;

> *2 Corinthians 2:2 (GNT) For while I was with you, I made up my mind to forget everything except Jesus Christ and especially his death on the cross.*

Why was this simple message so significant? Why the simplicity of it? It seems there were so many more things that He could have deemed worthy of greater or equal importance. Is this a complete message?

These are questions we have had in our journey, and ones we have heard from so many others. It's too easy to think; there has to be more. As a result, we often make it more complicated. Then, this simple message turns out to be not enough. This isn't new. This was true in Jesus' day as well. His followers struggled with it. The religious leaders rejected it. Others just dismissed it, or at best, included it along with everything else they were living for and worshipping.

The message Paul is preaching, and teaching is so powerful because it has finality built into it. With a proper reframe, we began to see how foundational this is. The rest of the tree grows because of the reality of this simple truth and message. It's a message of "once and for all." It's a message about completion. In the Words of Jesus Himself, "It is finished." In Aramaic, He would have said "tetelestai." Translated— it is finished; it is accomplished/completed. This truth can be so life-changing as you receive and embrace it. Let's dive in deeper.

IT IS FINISHED (Once & For All)

Finished: ended or completed; having all parts or elements; lacking nothing; whole; entire; full.

In Matthew 27:45-50, we read what Jesus went through as He was hanging on the cross. It is impossible to imagine the depth of grief and pain He suffered for and on our behalf (a.k.a. "substitutionary death"). Darkness came over the earth. At that moment, Jesus experienced a pain like no man has or will ever know— separation from His Father. That's when He cried out, *"Eli, Eli, lema sabachthani?"*—that is, "My God, My God, why have You forsaken Me?" Finally, Jesus cried out, took His last breath, and gave up His Spirit.

What part of "It Is Finished" were they struggling with? If you look a little deeper into this text, something interesting jumps out. Notice how The Religious and The Rebels responded. For them, Jesus wasn't the right person, and this was not the right plan. There had to be more. This could not be the One. He didn't fit the bill. He did not meet their expectations. For the followers of "The Way," the future appeared hopeless, and the end to everything they gave their lives for. It looked like defeat. For both of these, there was a struggle for proper perspective. There was tension regarding the future of their faith. What they were seeing was not complete (1 Corinthians 13:12).

In all fairness, you have to ask yourself the same question. What part of "It Is Finished" am I struggling with today? You have the rest of the story. You know what's on the other side (or you should anyway).

What is finished? Here's a look at some obvious things from the Old Covenant: scapegoats, sacrifices that were never enough, slavery to rituals, restricted and limited access to His presence, limited places of acceptable worship, guilt offering, sin offerings, accidental sin offerings, you even thought about being dumb offerings, looked at your momma wrong offerings, and on and on it goes.

You see, the death of The Messiah, Jesus the Christ, Son of The Living God means:

He has fulfilled the demands of the old covenant.

The power of sin is broken, and the sins of humanity paid in full— It is finished.

Sacrificial system complete and satisfied the Holy God that instituted it.

No more striving.

It was costly before (old covenant), and it has been paid.

The imperfect had to bring the best of the imperfect to be sacrificed in order to be accepted (as righteous) by God. The Perfect came from Heaven to offer the perfect sacrifice once and for all and establish righteousness by and through Himself.

Why His Death? Why was it necessary for the message to be what it is? First, it was to fulfill the prophecies, authenticating His identity, life & ministry. Secondly, it issued the proper payment— a propitiation (a fancy theological term for atonement) for man's sins. This was necessary for us to be reconciled back to God- to be in right relationship with Him. The first two people on earth broke this. So you can see why it's such a big deal. This message was talked about for thousands of years before Christ. The message? Jesus took the full payment for us to have a relationship with God as our Father for eternity.

Check out these lyrics from a years-past song by Ellis Crum that many grew up singing in the church. See if you can identify with this truth.

"He Paid a Debt He Did Not Owe"

He paid a debt He did not owe I owed a debt I could not pay I needed someone to wash my sins away. And now I sing a brand new song, Amazing Grace Christ Jesus paid a debt that I could never pay

My debt He paid upon the cross He cleansed my soul from all its dross I tho't that no one could all my sins erase. But now I sing a brand new song, Amazing Grace Christ Jesus paid a debt that I could never pay.

O such great pain my Lord endured When He my sinful soul secured I should have died there but Jesus took my place. So now I sing a brand new song, Amazing Grace Christ Jesus paid a debt that I could never pay

He didn't give to me a loan He gave Himself now He's my own He's gone to Heaven to make for me a place. And now I sing a brand new song Amazing Grace, Christ Jesus paid a debt that I could never pay.[25]

Lastly, the reason His death was necessary was that it released His provisions. Yes! It gave us access to a Holy God and all that's His. In the Old Covenant, we brought offerings and sacrifices to be accepted by God. Then Jesus gave Himself up as a ransom. And for those who believe and receive this message (as more than an academic exercise), they too have access to this New Covenant. Because of His body broken and blood shed (the perfect sacrifice), we have Eternal Life, access to God as our Father, hope, healing, acceptance, friendship and Intimacy with Jesus, the power, filling, and anointing of the Holy Spirit, and an invitation.

Believers and followers of Jesus: Remember. Celebrate. And for the love of all that is of God, let it be enough. It is finished. You're free to move from where you are. Get up and get out there and tell all who will listen about this Good News! Let's step up and into this excellent task of taking the message to the world. Why? Because we have experienced and are living in the reality of the great commandment. Like Peter, deny Him no longer. Be restored if you have. Walk in your new identity!

The Rebel and The Curious: Wait no longer. The day of salvation is at hand. Receive this message of eternal hope!

2 Corinthians 6:2 (ESV) For He says, "In a favorable time I listened to you, and in a day of salvation I have helped you."

Psalm 95:7-8 (ESV) For He is our God, and we are the people of His pasture, and the sheep of His hand. Today, if you hear His voice, do not harden your hearts...

---

25   Crum, Ellis J., *"He Paid A Debt He Did Not Owe,"* Ellis J. Crum, Publisher (Admin. by Sacred Selections R.E. Winsett LLC), 1977.

Hebrews 3:7-8 (TPT) 7 This is why the Holy Spirit says, "If only you would listen to His voice this day! 8 Don't make Him angry by hardening your hearts, like your ancestors did during the days of their rebellion, when they were tested in the wilderness.

It Is Finished! So, let's get started! We have the message. Let's be carriers of this good news, missionaries to everyone, wherever we live.

GOOD NEWS REQUIRES A RESPONSE

The message is what we are carrying and fulfilling in the mission. Have you ever thought about what living in alignment with His vision looks like (collectively as the church)? Remember, it always starts with individuals, and bears fruit as the body of believers walk together in obedience. Where do you think you are in your alignment regarding the following items:

- The Great Commandment (Mark 12:30-31)?
- Experiencing, reciprocating and passing on His grace and love?
- Prayer being a driving force for living (relationally and practically)?
- Using spiritual gifts for the growth, health and unity of the body?

If you found yourselves lacking in any of these areas, it might be time for a reframe.

Challenge: pray and ask God to awaken your heart and reframe your mind to the reality and importance of the message— the Good News! Here are a few passages that can get you excited about the message. When you read them, ask the Holy Spirit to give you wisdom and discernment that you would know how to live in response to them.

Romans 6:23 / Ephesians 2:13 / John 1:1, 3:16

CHAPTER 11

THE CHURCH - PART 3

"THE MISSIONARIES"

WHO ARE MISSIONARIES?

Are missionaries those people who live in jungles far far away? Are they the weird people who show up now and then to your church and give you a report as to all the awesome things God is doing all over the world? Are missionaries the ones that get to see all the cool stuff of God that the rest of us commoners here in America aren't privy to?

Depending on your upbringing, one or more of those questions probably entered your mind at some point. What if we told you that every believer and follower of Christ is called to be a missionary? It's true. Sure, there are of course those that God has called out to serve at this level vocationally.

However, this is not about the occupation. This is about the challenge and charge given everyone one of Christ's followers.

We are the sent ones. The ambassadors. The missionaries of the Message. The carrier of the Good News.

> MISSIONARY - What is a missionary? Jesus gives these words here;
>
> *John 20:21 (AMP) Then Jesus said to them again, "Peace to you; as the Father has sent Me, I also send you [as My representatives]."*

Oswald Chambers says it like this;

> "A missionary is someone sent by Jesus Christ just as He was sent by God. The great controlling factor is not the needs of people, but the command of Jesus."[26]

As missionaries, we are called to live and carry a simple message. It's a message that even a child can both live and share. What about doctrines— aren't they important? Of course, they are. We have hopefully established that in two chapters before this one. Since we have one mission, One who has sent us, one message to give, then it stands to reason that we should also be one as a team, family, the church. In some ways, we have seen a significant number of different churches, mission agencies and ministries all function (for better and worse) separately for so long. This has made it easy to draw deep and unnecessary lines in the sand. Consequently, many have made, in many cases, unnecessary and unhealthy divisions. Much of this is created by how and why we label things as major and minor.

It sounds like it should be easy to major and minor on the things the way Jesus did. If you're anything like us, we looked deeper and found that it was much easier said than done (practically speaking). You see, Jesus wasn't focusing on gifts of the Spirit, spiritual gifts, types of churches, particulars of doctrinal and theological bents, etc. So why is it so easy for us to get trapped into focusing on ourselves? Why do we get

---

26   Chambers, Oswald, *"My Utmost For His Highest,"* Kindle location 5446 of 6786, Third Edition, Discovery House, 2017.

wrapped around the axle on the minor things and cause great division at the expense of the things that matter most?

Here is what makes this so messy— we are all humans; we hear from the Holy Spirit at different levels and unique places in life; we all have varied experiences, education, and training that create filters in our ability to understand the Word of God the way we do entirely. Some are scared of this. Some are threatened by this, even to the point where they would call us heretics for not fully aligning in their complete understanding of all their various perspectives and paradigms of doctrines and disciplines.

If we are indeed the bride of Christ, then we are an apostolic people (sent ones). Kris Vallotton often says that churches were born out of covenant, not a conference or convention (as it pertains to the New Testament Churches). Apostolic people are covenant people. There is one covenant. There is one body.

Speaking of getting wrapped around the axle and confusing majors and minors— here are some of the things that make our skin crawl a little bit (theological jargon that is not actual Biblical terminology);

Cessationism vs Continuationism

Calvinism vs Arminianism

Complimentarianism vs Egalitarianism

Fundamentalism vs Modernism

Denomination vs Non-denominationa

Reformed vs Non-Reformed

Evangelical vs Protestant

Liberal vs Conservative

Progressive vs Traditional

Big Church vs Home or Small Church

These are camps of sorts created by man, for man. These often become identities instead of frameworks for understanding any particular position. Many times over these have created factions and sides of any given perspective in the Bible and life in general. There is so much more than trying to identify with one camp over another. Believe it or not, you can have a particular bent based on your walk with Jesus and time in His Word without being labeled or relegated to a specific camp. These are the very schisms that Jesus died to break down, permanently. And, these are not identities for missionaries on a mission with Jesus.

The list goes on and on. We have created such a great divide, and many have staked their lives on them. In the end, we are unwise to place the stamp of God on any one of these types of identities since all of them are man's attempts to nicely package Biblical doctrines and disciplines, theological positions and postures, as well as the practical pieces of life and liberty for followers of Jesus. Once again, this was never the approach Jesus took in teaching and training His followers. God does not look at each of us and characterize us as missionaries within these man-made classifications. It's our position that none of these should ever be how you define yourself.

You might say, "what about all the instruction that Paul gave the church regarding doctrines and disciplines, positions and postures, life and liberty?" Lest this get in the way of our methodology, it would suffice to say that Paul was never trying to create a system and methodology through these things. These were all to protect the one thing that mattered most to Paul— knowing, believing, and following Jesus Christ as well as making Him known.

So, here we are. You can see why a major reframe might be in order when it comes to who we are as missionaries. We were called to be one. One is not the loneliest number. If it is, it's only to the extent that you are on your own, or disconnected in the midst of many. Another way you know there's a need for a reframe is when any one group thinks they've figured it all out and have become exclusive to those who align with their particular bent and flavor. We can't even begin to explain how problematic this is for the bride of Christ.

One is an easy number until it involves more than one. Let us explain. Looking out for #1 seems to be the default for humanity. It is in our human nature to look primarily at our own interests.

Is Unity Important?

Another great perspective from Francis Chan comes from the story in 1 Timothy concerning two men who rejected the faith. He goes on to say;

> "Paul said that he had handed them over to Satan, by which he meant that he'd put them outside of the church (1:20). Basically, these men were actively opposing the works of God, so rather than pretending everything was fine, Paul removed them from the safety and blessings of the fellowship of believers. He was hoping that the misery of being separated from the church would lead them to repent."[27]

In Jesus Name

When two or more are gathered, if the two of you are walking in the Spirit (oneness with each other and the Holy Spirit), you will ask according to the Spirit, and He can then answer this prayer. If two or more are walking in the Spirit, you are agreeing to what He is saying, and He will provide for what He is saying.

When it comes to unity, we must fight against the ever-growing list of things that can and are dividing us.

CRACKS - CREVASSE - CHASM

As you can see, even the most minor of cracks in this foundation (unity in/with Christ by the power of the Holy Spirit for the glory of God) creates crevasses. Left unchecked, these become catastrophic chasms, bringing down even the greatest of people, families, churches, and nations.

We Are One

One Easter weekend, we witnessed the culmination of hours of preparation and sacrifice from members of at least six

---

27   Chan, Francis, "*Letters To The Church*," Kindle location 825 of 2302, David C. Cook, Crazy Love Ministries, 2018.

different local bodies of Christ at work. All of this was for our annual Community Easter Service. We saw first hand what Scripture describes as "one body with many members." Even more so, we were honored to experience so many members using their uniquely crafted, God-given gifts! Paul (the apostle) explains this supernatural phenomenon within the local body of Christ known as "the church."

> *1 Corinthians 12:4-7 (TPT) 4 It is the same Holy Spirit who continues to distribute many different varieties of gifts. 5 The Lord Yahweh is One, and He is the One who apportions to believers different varieties of ministries. 6 The same God distributes different kinds of miracles that accomplish different results through each believer's gift and ministry as he energizes and activates them. 7 Each believer is given continuous revelation by the Holy Spirit to benefit not just himself but all.*

Friends, there are many structures throughout any given town where the children of God reside. In our story above, we realized that the walls themselves didn't change a single heart that Easter weekend. It was the power of the Holy Spirit pouring through the faithful servants of God who listened to His prompting to serve, obeyed His voice, and put their hands and feet to the task of serving each other. This is what made a world of difference in the community. And guess what? God brought great blessing TO His people THROUGH His people!

All those who buckled down for hours of planning sacrificed time with their families and committed to following Jesus' example of serving others allowed for Jesus' Perfect and Holy name to be lifted high and glorified in this community. The people of God working together, side by side, let us all worship as ONE body truly! Everyone's effort indeed ushered in a manifestation of the Holy Spirit for the common good of all Christ-followers in the community. And friends, this is what made that weekend so very special! We experienced the very presence of God through His Spirit, flowing out from the hands and feet of His servants.

May we strive every day to focus on lifting Jesus high in

our own hearts, as well as out in our community. Together, as one body, let's consider this truth found here;

> *Romans 12:4-5 (NLT) 4 Just as our bodies have many parts and each part has a special function, 5 so it is with Christ's body. We are many parts of one body, and we all belong to each other.*

ONE MIND

Why do we hear these words in scripture "Be of one mind" yet run from it in church? We allow fear to drive us into corrupt practices. We have heard people in churches say things like, "Well, we don't want our leader just to pick leaders that think like him/her." That's foolish to us. Where the thinking comes from and what it's focused on is the more significant issue. If we are to have the mind of Christ (Philippians 2:5), then our goal should always be for our minds to be alike. This requires extreme humility and selflessness. Side note: please do not assume this means we can't or shouldn't have different ideas, opinions, thoughts, and perspectives.

Our time here on earth in this life is a short one. This should be an essential theme and reality for your life. It will positively affect the way you think, live and love. We don't have the luxury of looking at any day as a waste or a write-off. Every day is important and effects the remaining days we have left.

Jesus knew His time was short as well when He was here in His earthly body. This is why He was so set on making sure everything He did was directly from His Father. It's why He spent so much time with Him, seeking Him, hearing Him, and doing as He said. His Father never contradicted the written Scriptures. Jesus walked with His Father in a way that led every step He took. Thankfully, Jesus modeled this for us, giving us the proper way to both follow and lead (follow Him and lead/serve others in our areas of governance/influence).

What's the point of all that? You might think if you haven't spent a great deal of time in the Bible, that the plan and process is a complicated one. It's not. Because it's so simple, it's often overlooked and ignored. We often live our lives in a way that does not make room for simplicity. He gives us one thing, and we add a few more, then a few more, then a few more. Then, with great exhaustion, we tell God that it's just too hard. The sad reality and evidence of all this is the people who are living complicated, self-destructive, defeated, shameful, sinful, guilt-ridden lives. And, to make things worse— IT WILL NOT WORK! So, what is it then?

Oneness. Yes! Oneness. You can already see why this is a battle from the very beginning. This might be the very thing that God can use to change the trajectory of your life. I can speak with authority on this because the Bible says it's true. And I believe the Bible. Simple, right? It all works better when we are one (together).

> One- being a single unit or thing; being the same in kind or quality; constituting a unified entity of two or more components (the combined elements form one substance); being in agreement or union.[28]

This means that all the individual pieces and parts that are not together are only "one" within themselves.

"One" isn't without the capability of being different. It's like the body. God has given us this example in the Bible to understand this better. You have two eyes. Two ears. One mouth. One nose. Two arms and hands. Two legs and feet. Now, imagine what happens when they all go separate ways. If you have ever found yourself tumbling down the mountain like a slinky with a pair of skis strapped to your feet, then you understand this phenomenon. It' doesn't work well. There is no fruit from it, just chaos and confusion (and a lot of aches and pains).

You want to know how big a deal this is to Jesus? Many of you are familiar with the High Priestly Prayer offered by Jesus in John 17:1-26. Jesus prayed for unity and oneness in these three areas:

#1 - (One) In The Godhead (17:1-5). First, Jesus prayed for

---

28   Merriam-Webster Online Dictionary, copyright by Merriam-Webster, Incorporated, www.merriam-webster.com, 2015, https://www.merriam-webster.com/dictionary/one.

Himself, He knew that He needed to be in alignment with the Father before anything else. He had to be ONE with the Creator in order for there to be a ONENESS with the created. First word— "Father."

Then He says, "The hour has come." God's divine plan of redemption was here and in place. "Glorify Your Son" would ultimately be glorifying God Himself. Remember, the ultimate goal of all mankind is to glorify God (1 Corinthians 10:31).

#2 - (One) In The Body (17:6-19). This particular part of His prayer was for the apostles. Even so, this applies to all believers/followers of Jesus. Remember, we are in places where we will either serve best by leading and at other times lead best by serving. However, in order to be consistent with Scripture, Jesus prays the words recorded in this passage for His apostles.

They believed in Jesus' mission and obeyed God's Word. He prayed for their protection here in this world (verse 11). The only way that would be possible is if they remained as one, as Jesus and the Father are one. Otherwise, they would be easy targets and play into the enemy's hand and plan. He prayed that their joy would be fulfilled (verses 12-19). This would only happen if they: operate as "ONE," are kept from the evil one, are sanctified in the Truth (God's Word), and are fulfilling their mission.

#3 - (One) In The Mission (17:20-26). The mission would never change. The message would not change. The mode would not change (it would always be His people). However, the methodology would continue to change. It changed from church to church in the Bible and has not stopped morphing in over two thousand years. That's bad news if you're not big on change, but great news for all those out there who have not been reached yet. They are our mission. Out there! If this were not so, it would have been much easier for Jesus just to put up a shingle and start His own mega-church in His home town.

Jesus' mission was to bring the transformational truth by the powerful work of the Holy Spirit to many more after Him. This was the very work He left His followers to continue until His return (v. 20). Notice that this still happens in the context of being and working as one. The centrality of the ONE is first and foremost the Messiah, Savior, Jesus the Christ— Son of the Living God (verses 21-23).

As missionaries, when we function as one bride, one family, one church, we will reap a great harvest together. We see this reflected in this tremendous and hopeful summary in verses 24-26.

This is how it happens in the Family, the Body, the Bride, the Church. First, you have to be in oneness with the Father, Son, and Holy Spirit. Then, you need to be in oneness with those within the church. Lastly, you are called to be in oneness with the mission of the church.

Every believer has been given roles and the responsibilities that accompany those roles. Any time God grants this, He also undergirds it with the appropriate (by the Holy Spirit) authority to carry it out. That means that you have an area of life that you are to govern and steward. You have a massive part in the Kingdom, a significant role with all the responsibilities that go with it.

Now, here's where it gets a little heavy— stay with us. When you do not step into the role that God has placed you in, fulfill the responsibilities that role carries, and govern well with the authority God has given you, you will by default try and exercise that authority in areas that are not yours. This is a problem of epidemic proportions in local churches throughout our country.

REFRAME: THE PEOPLE

With everything going on in our society, it's incredible to us that Jesus still loves His church the way He does. The amazement is not so much why He would love her, but how He continues to love her. If you grew up in church, chances are your frame of reference regarding the church at large is confined to the local church experience you spent time in.

On a personal note— throughout the years we have been serving in ministry, there have been numerous times where we were ready not to be involved with the local church at the staff/leadership level. We wanted to do something else (for God of course), just not in/with/through the church. The church as we knew it was not cutting it.

As we learned to reframe this through prayer, God's Word and wise counsel, it became much more clear that this was still God's primary vehicle in reaching the world with the Gospel of Jesus Christ. So, now when people run into all the other opportunities to impact people, my question is, "What about the church?"

The perfect church— it's for sure not a place or organizational structure. It's more of a mindset and spirit (that calls us into oneness and unity). What are we looking for in "The Perfect Church?" What should be our approach to the church? The church at large has spent so long trying to design a place that fits the "needs" of the people, and somehow have lost the discipline for, and dependency on, the wisdom that comes not from our understanding, but that which can only come through the Holy Spirit.

If we are going to reach our communities and nations for Christ, and make any difference whatsoever, the church must be: REAL - RELEVANT - RELATIONAL

PRINCIPLE VERSUS PRACTICE (BEING A BIBLICAL CHURCH)

Maybe you have heard the churches in the New Testament referred to as the "Early Church." We are not the early church. We are the church of the last days. One of the potential dangers we have as modern day missionaries is trying to mimic the early church (especially without knowing and understanding the historical context). For so many, this has caused somewhat of a crippling identity crisis.

There are apparent struggles and tensions within the life of churches today to be the "New Testament Church" and still operate as a corporate structure (as the world has defined it). This causes us to live such duplicitous lives. We say it's not about the buildings and programs, but we end up being so driven by them. They tend to own us more than we can use them.

People at large are seeking organic relationships, not organized religion. As missionaries in the local church, we must be careful not to confuse trading caught fish with catching fresh fish— recycling versus new. The church that sells herself and her products becomes a business and creates consumers. What else can we expect?

REFRAME: THE PEOPLE (COVENANT RELATIONSHIP VS CHURCH MEMBERSHIP)

God created you and chose to move and operate in a relationship with you by way of covenants. Our position regarding covenants is not in total alignment with Covenant Theology. That being said, the only way to be in covenant relationship with each other is to first be in covenant relationship with God (the Author and Maintainer of the covenant). This is all made possible because of the great work Jesus accomplished on the cross and the powerful work of the Holy Spirit in and through your lives.

> **COVENANT**: (noun) agreement; undertaking; commitment; guarantee; warrant; pledge; promise; bond; indenture; pact; deal, settlement, arrangement, understanding. (verb) contract, guarantee, pledge, promise, agree, engage, warrant, commit oneself, bind oneself. [Theology] An agreement that brings about a relationship of commitment between God and His people.

> **MEMBERSHIP**: (noun) the fact of being a member of a group; belonging to a social group, or company as a member.

In 1 Thessalonians 1:1-10, Paul was so thankful for these people. A church that will pray together and serve together will almost always stay together. It was what they did together. They worked hard (together) because of faith in "in our Lord Jesus Christ." It was their shared faith that made serving the one living and true God worth the hard work. And, they already knew of His example.

Don't miss the laboring and toiling (together) because of their love for Jesus. They were able to do this even in the middle of persecution (verse 6). This love for Jesus makes joy possible even in the midst of laboring and toiling. This is reserved for the Deo-centric life (God-centered) and not the ego-centric life (self-centered). They endured (together) under pressure because of their hope in Christ (verse 10).

They knew the outcome.

Being an example was a high priority. Following their leaders as their leaders followed Christ was critical to their fulfillment. They set the example for others to follow as well (like the domino effect). The results were amazing. They experienced joy because of the supernatural work of the Holy Spirit. They gave what they were given (the Gospel message). The life-changing Gospel drove them to provide it to others. They participated in global outreach, not just local. Their work and word of their work spread throughout the land. They responded to the Holy Spirit and changed. They turned from idols to the One True God. They lived with great belief, confidence, and hope. This was their reframe!

It makes it pretty obvious that these were great people to be around. Their hard work and sacrifice was noticed and appreciated by so many. The joy that came from their lives of faith, hope and love was infectious and life-changing.

Part of the problem/challenge in the local church today is we have people that are not in covenant relationship with God or His people, but members of a local religious group at best. This is supposed to be a practical, living, growing relationship. A healthy family loves unconditionally. Intimately. Through thick and thin. You don't give up on each other because you don't like something or you have changing feelings. Family relationships— they were never supposed to be broken. So when they are, it makes sense why it's so traumatic.

Contracts and promises can be broken pretty easily. Often times there is little to no fall out over them. Western society has become so jaded that the conversation seems to carry a whole different weight than it did 20, 30, 50, 75 years ago. Our culture is so fractured that even the way you receive this and process will be different than the next reader. This is why a Biblical worldview has to always be our plumb line, our center, and our compass.

If we understand the nuclear family, we can better understand the value of the local family of God. Just like we have extended family living in other houses all over the place, the same is true for homes of faith. Being a member of anything other than the family is more about me— my music, book, food, gyms, clubs and anything else interest based. It's not about my interest. It's about His interest. Membership is about you. Covenant relationship is about Jesus.

Covenant relationship with God through Christ is the only way we are to live. Being in covenant relationship with Jesus translates into serving Him by serving those He created. It would stand to reason then that the follower of Christ who is connected to a local body of believers is experiencing maturity and growth in a way those detached cannot. And, the local church is still the model, mode, and method God desires to use. Even though studies show that over 80% of Christians believe it's not necessary to be connected with a local church to have a growing relationship with God, those of us who are know differently.

THE MISSIONARY MINDSET

The majority of the NT is all about living within the context of missional community (the local church). What instruction or encouragement is God giving you that needs to be fleshed out in the context of the local church?

As a part of a healthy reframe, identifying those unhealthy relationships you've had with improper alignment or false identities is critical to a more abundant life in Christ. Ask the Holy Spirit to help bring those to the light, and release them. Then, ask Him to help you better understand who you are in Christ, and what He is calling you deeper into as a missionary (a follower of Christ in mission).

Remember, it's impossible to experience the fullness of God in covenant relationship apart from the local church. The church is how/who God desires to work and move through to complete His Kingdom work here on earth. Disconnecting from the church is forfeiting blessings, covering, anointing, and numerous other workings of the Holy Spirit. Ask God to increase your desire to find and be a part of a healthy church family. This kind of reframe will be more fulfilling than you could imagine!

For a more in-depth look at what it means to walk in unity for the greater good, take a look at some of these passages:

John 20:19-24 (Jesus Commissioning The Disciples)

Acts 1:8 (Power For Purpose)

Ephesians 4:1-16 (Unity In The Body of Christ)

Philippians 2:1-11 (Christ's Example Of Humility)

CHAPTER 12

THE CHURCH - PART 4

PART 4 - "THE METHODS"

CHICKEN OR EGG?

Which came first? The chicken or the egg? This is much like the ongoing debate between theology and methodology. There are a few churches that we have seen that are not in this battle. Maybe if we spent more time sharpening our theology, we would find less time for divisiveness and attack in each other's methodology.

What are the right methods and means, tool and plans, in reaching the world with the good news of Jesus Christ? Well, that depends on who you ask, what church you go to, what denomination you belong to, what side of the fence you're on, what books you are reading, what communicators you're listening to, and maybe even what you had for breakfast. Good grief. How in the world did we get here? Ha! Before you beat yourself up about it (or someone else), know that it's not new. It was present even in the early church.

When we look back at the early church in the New Testament, we read about the apostle Paul writing so much to the churches with correction, instruction and even rebuke. Why? Mainly, because they kept forgetting to keep the main thing the main thing— Jesus Christ crucified (1 Corinthians 1:23-24). Jesus was all about seeking to save that lost (Luke 19:10).

He came as The Bread of Life and The Living Water. This is what we should be concerned about giving people. And, similar to being in a disaster relief area, we should do whatever we can to get them this Bread of Life and Living Water. It seems that one of our most significant hurdles in Western Culture is our lacking awareness and/or our ignorance (willful or otherwise) towards the severity of the ongoing natural disaster we live in. Fact— people are dying without the saving knowledge of Jesus Christ. Worse— as people starve to death spiritually all around us and around the world, we are seeing far too much spiritual food sitting in the pantries of our churches and houses.

Why the rant? Glad you asked. We are in a fantastic place and position in history to take this message of hope all over the world like never before. Jesus has given us some incredible gems in the Bible to steer us in our individual and corporate methodology. Let's not spend all our time splitting hairs at the expense of getting this Living Bread and Water to all those who need it. What we're not saying is that every method and practice of telling people about God's love is acceptable. Many have done deplorable things in the name of God's love. So, every method is not healthy or honoring to Jesus and His message of love and salvation.

STRUCTURE

We want to give two primary perspectives here— one from the Old Testament and one from the New Testament. The structure is so important, but it has unfortunately created so much confusion and hatred in the church. We hope this will shed a little light on why this reframe is so important.

In 2 Chronicles 5-7, we see four primary action points regarding "structure."

First: The Preparation (the ark at the center of the temple— God's Word)

Second: The Prayer (Solomon prays)

Third: The Presence (God shows up)

Fourth: The Promise (God responds to Solomon's prayer with a promise)

King David, the greatest king Israel had ever known, had a desire to build God a house. God was pleased, but His house would need a pure foundation. David had seen too much war and shed too much blood. God honored his dream by promising David that his son (Solomon) would build it. David then made painstaking preparations. He made plans for the temple, gathered all the materials, built relationships with vendors, made instruments for worship and stored up Holy vessels of gold and silver. He arranged everything for his son so he could fulfill the plans God had for him.

Then, Solomon rose into place, and the temple was built. A man of peace, by God's description. The foundation of the temple was laid on the hard work and preparation of David and under the direction of a man of peace. Once it was built, Solomon gathered all the elders and the people at the beginning of the seventh month, the annual feast of tabernacles.

The first order of business we see in chapter 5 was to bring the ark into the center of the structure. God's Word needed to be in its rightful place, at the heart of the structure. So the Levites (they were the priests) brought the ark in.

Next came sacrifice. Both the king and people sacrificed before the ark so many offerings they could not be counted. As the people brought their sacrifices, the priests stood at their given posts and offered praises, songs, and thanksgiving. As they brought sacrifice and praise, the cloud filled the temple so that the priests could no longer stand. The presence of God was so thick they couldn't even stand!

Then, in chapter 6, Solomon stands and acknowledges God's presence, and begins to pray. He first reminds the people they are standing in a moment where God is fulfilling His promise to David. God promised his son would be on the throne and promised his son would build a house for His presence. He acknowledges the whole moment is due to a plan, promise, and provisions from God.

He then asks that God's eyes and ears would ever be present, seeing the people, hearing and honoring their fervent prayers as they looked toward the temple in the time of need. He asks God to answer their prayer and meet their needs no matter what issues they were facing.

Lastly, in chapter 7 we see God's direct response to Solomon's prayer of intercession for the people and his prayer of dedication for the temple. Once Solomon finished praying, asking for God to see them and hear them, and respond, God, answers with fire. Fire fell and consumed the countless sacrifices that were just made by the multitude. And the glory of the Lord filled the temple.

When the people saw the fire fall from heaven, they went face down in worship and Thanksgiving, acknowledging God's goodness and faithfulness. God responded to their prayer, and the people responded to God. This is what the temple was all about. God promised that IF indeed His people would be humble, pray, seek Him, and turn from their wicked ways, He would hear them and respond accordingly, just as Solomon had requested.

This method of putting God's Word first and bringing Him into the center of the structure was a game changer. They brought sacrifices and offerings, continual praise and worship as well as fervent prayer for the people and their many needs. God listened and responded. And the people responded in even more praise, worship, and thanksgiving.

The structure wasn't about a physical structure at all. The right structure was a culmination of plans, preparation, sacrifice, praise, and prayer which resulted in the presence of God's glory. The structure is about a place of restoring relationship with God, coming clean and acknowledging their need. It's not God's home, but it is a temple that He is willing to fill with His glory.

Now for the New Testament perspective. Let's look at what Jesus did leave us in regards to structure for God's people. First, a look at the church. Jesus was many things, but here are five that are of great importance to the church and her health. These five come primarily from Ephesians 4. There are many supporting passages to go with each of these, but we have only listed one for each to keep the emphasis on Jesus as the Great;

APOSTLE

Hebrews 3:1 (ESV) Therefore, holy brothers, you who share in a heavenly calling, consider Jesus, the apostle and high priest of our confession...

PROPHET

Luke 7:16 (ESV) Fear seized them all, and they glorified God, saying, "A great prophet has arisen among us!" and "God has visited his people!"

EVANGELIST

John 3:16-17 (ESV) 16 For God so loved the world, that he gave his only Son, that whoever believes in him should not perish but have eternal life. 17 For God did not send his Son into the world to condemn the world, but in order that the world might be saved through Him.

SHEPHERD/PASTOR

John 10:14-16 (ESV) 14 I am the good shepherd. I know my own and my own know me, 15 just as the Father knows me and I know the Father; and I lay down my life for the sheep. 16 And I have other sheep that are not of this fold. I must bring them also, and they will listen to my voice. So there will be one flock, one shepherd.

TEACHER

John 7:14-17 (TPT) 14 Not until the feast was half over did Jesus finally appear in the temple courts and begin to teach. 15 The Jewish leaders were astonished by what he taught and said, "How did this man acquire such knowledge? He wasn't trained in our schools—who taught him?" 16 So Jesus responded, "I don't teach my own ideas, but the truth revealed to me by the One who sent me. 17 If you want to test my teachings and discover where I received them, first be passionate to do God's will, and then you will be able to discern if my teachings are from the heart of God or from my own opinions.

So, as it pertains to the health and effectiveness of the church, we must see these characteristics of Christ reflected in and through it. This is why Paul gave us these instructions;

Ephesians 4:11 (TPT) And he has appointed some with grace to be apostles, and some with grace to be prophets, and some with grace to be evangelists, and some with grace to be pastors, and some with grace to be teachers.

If we want to see the fullness of Christ manifested in the church, why in the world would we choose to remove any part of who He is from it? Yes, plenty believe that this is no longer applicable to today's church. That's baffling to us. However, it is understandable why they have chosen to believe this way considering all the misuse and abuse of these roles and responsibilities.

Let's think about that a little more. Did Jesus provide the church an assortment of corporate titles like CEO? President? Board Member? Officer? No! Jesus did not leave the church titles and positions. He left the church roles and responsibilities.

Our personal story is, for so long we were taught and saw modeled this idea that "pastor" is an all-inclusive position, title, role, and responsibility that was given to those who are "called." Although exhausting, it sounded fine- until we collapsed under its pressure and were driven back to Scripture for help and healing. Then, we could not find that all-in-one mindset anywhere in the Bible apart from Jesus Himself.

We found just the opposite to be true. Ephesians 4 was actually the standard and not the exception. It was not relegated to the first/early church (New Testament Church). What Jesus left the church was not just for the first church, but the church at large, today!

Again, so that there is no confusion (if that's possible), these roles and responsibilities that are given in Ephesians 4:11 were not provided for people to run empires with titles and VIP badges with entourages. Ha! Can you picture it? Is Jesus walking around with the disciples as His bodyguards? If anything, it would be the other way around. Right? Alright, stop laughing and let's get back to it. These roles and responsibilities were given for two reasons: 1) As grace gifts to the body. 2) To activate the other gifts in the body.

> *Ephesians 4:12 (ESV) ...to equip the saints for the work of ministry, for building up the body of Christ...*

See? The APEST (Apostle/Prophet/Evangelist/Shepherd/Teacher) model was not given to rule the world. This was given to serve the body in a way that would open the fullness of ministry opportunities for each believer in the body of Christ. It's the ministry of the body that Paul tells us will enlarge and build up the body of Christ. The plan was never about a one-man-band. It was never about a select few conquering communities and countries in Jesus' name. It was the plan from the very beginning for the Holy Spirit to move through the body as a whole! That's why it is so critically important that each of us is serving in a body of believers, using the gifts, abilities, and talents God has given us.

If you're wondering why this is important, take a look at the rest of what Paul says in chapter four. In verses 13-15, Paul says the grace gifts will all continue to function until we all attain oneness in the faith and experience the fullness of what it means to know Jesus. Only when we reach full maturity and be fully developed in the abundance of Christ will the gifts be no longer. Our maturity will be complete. The end of this passage says, "All our direction and ministries will flow from Christ and lead us deeper into Him, the anointed Head of His body, the church."

GIFTS

If we stick with Ephesians 4 (although there are so many additional passages we could dive into regarding this), Paul continues to describe the body of believers that Christ has put together, and what makes that body work together at the highest level. Verse 16 describes a body that is continually being joined together and connected as one. Each of these members of the body has gifts, and they only operate effectively when they do so together. The results of these gifts in motion are the body / church built up in love and made perfect in love. When is the last time you've seen this? Praise God if and when you have.

You see how important those APEST gifts were to the body. Can you see just how important the rest of the gifts are? How important are you to the body? How important each of our roles and responsibilities is to the work of God's plan?

So why don't we see this more in the church today? Why are more people not using the gifts and abilities God has given them? The more extended version of this answer is another series of books (maybe called "All the Excuses in the World"). But in short, we believe there are a few main reasons.

The first reason we find most common is ignorance. The unfortunate reality is, many Christians don't know. They have not been taught. They have not been discipled. This is sad for us. And, this speaks to a bigger challenge in the church regarding the way we disciple within the body (or the way we don't). Ignorance is an easy one to fix. The highest commission given us was to make disciples. So, if you've not been discipled, find a more mature believer than you and ask them to disciple you. If you are a seasoned or maturing believer, find someone to disciple. Nailed it! It's not much more complicated than that.

Another primary reason for the lack of gifts exercised in the church is disobedience. This is the hardest one for us to conceive. God the Father sent the Son to save you. You received that gift, and now you're free. However, can you imagine refusing to allow the Holy Spirit to accomplish the ongoing work of freedom in your life? Are you kidding? That's nothing less than self-sabotage. This is not what Christ set you free for.

Galatians 5:1 (NIV) says, "It is for freedom that Christ has set us free."

Another area we have to address regarding spiritual gifts is jealousy and discontentment. We have seen over the years this struggle in the local church where people have sought after positions of power and authority. That's bad, but it only gets worse when they mask as a desire to serve out of their gifts. It's quite easy for each of us to be jealous of another's gifts when we see God using people different than ourselves. It's easy for us to be envious of another person's success and favor when we feel we are equally or more deserving. It's here that the phrase "stay in your lane" comes to mind.

1 Corinthians 7:17-24 is a power-packed reframe that can help us be faithful and content with what He is doing in us and has provided for us. Take a look at three particular verses in this passage (but read the whole thing later for further study and context).

1 Corinthians 7:17, 20, 24 (ESV) 17 Only let each person lead the life that the Lord has assigned to him, and to which God has called him. This is my rule in all the churches... 20 Each one should remain in the condition in which he was called. 24 So, brothers, in whatever condition each was called, there let him remain with God.

Speaking of being faithful with the lot you've got, there is a verse in Proverbs 28 that has rocked our worlds. It is a firm foundation for us in times of confusion and doubt. Check it out.

Proverbs 28:19 (ESV) Whoever works his land will have plenty of bread, but he who follows worthless pursuits will have plenty of poverty.

What jumped off the page here was the phrase "works HIS land." God the Father gives us as His children our portion in life. His provision to us is our sphere to work for His glory. A land to cultivate with His goodness through us. The critical question here is, are we faithful in the land which Jesus has placed us? Are we faithful to get up and put our hands to the plow whether we're tired or excited, whether in season or out of season, whether the land is cooperating or not? Are we faithful to work our own land? Are we following trivial pursuits which would, by default, be attempting to work someone else's land? Do we long for another portion, another lot, another sphere? If we aren't faithful at the plow right where we are, we certainly won't be faithful to plow where we aren't!

This verse comes with a fantastic promise: When we faithfully steward the lot we've got, there'll always be something in our pot! We are promised we will have plenty of bread. The Word does not say we will have large nightly feasts in our towering mansions. But it does say plenty of bread—we will be provided for. We won't be neglected. The faithful hand at the plow will see plenty of bread in it at meal time. However, this understanding of plenty is defined by God, not you or me.

When Paul was in prison or even traveling, he often went hungry and was thirsty. He knew what it was like to not have some of the things we would identify as the essentials. Even then, he said he was content because in Christ he was technically not in need (Philippians 4:10-20).

Perhaps we should stop wishing for another field and start working, plowing, sowing, watering, and clearing the field we've got. Wishing for something else only brings contempt for what you have and covetousness for what others have. If you spend your time gazing at another field, you'll neglect the one you're in, and come up empty at meal time. The dissatisfaction internally will lead to dissatisfaction externally. The internal lack will lead to external lack. But if we are abundantly inwardly satisfied with our Father, and trust He's placed us in the right field at the right time, we will show faithfulness to care for our field and reap a rich reward externally.

The methodology seems to be a significant source of division and has been throughout the generations. In fact, it's often the cloak and dagger operation behind drawing lines that become chasms in the fellowship of the believers. Part of the way we flesh out a healthy mission is with healthy methods. The method is not about the promotion of any particular person or perspective. Those aren't methods; they're mindsets. They are personal perspectives. They are often the very tool the enemy uses to keep us from operating as a unified family.

This is not an issue of a big church, a small church or even home church. Corporate gatherings for worship can be infinite in size. That's just what it is— corporate worship. The greater conversation is not how big our gatherings are, but how personal and effective the true church of Christ is living in authentic community.

As the church, we need to avoid being in the way of showing people The Way. Our challenge as the church is to stop creating more obstacles for those who would come to know the Lord (Acts 15:19). Stop inventing more rules and regulations like the religious leaders did in the early church (and continues to this day). Start tearing down the high places. Start turning our hearts towards God, then leading others likewise. We cannot lead people to a place where we are not. We cannot teach or help people use their gifts effectively if we are not using our own correctly.

Do you know what your spiritual gifts are? Are you using them? There is a difference between spiritual gifts and gifts of the Spirit. However, if you believe the same Holy Spirit possesses those gifts, and if you have the Spirit, then do you not also have access to those gifts? Spiritual gifts can often cause division in the church family. Paul wanted to make some things clear about them. We see this in his first letter to the Corinthians.

Where do they come from? 1 Corinthians 12:1-8,11 answers that question. We must start here. So much of the confusion and abuse regarding spiritual gifts begins here. Paul starts off telling the church that he did not want them to go on being uninformed, or misinformed. He wanted them to know that it is the work of the Holy Spirit in their lives that even allowed them to say with personal conviction "Jesus is Lord."

Paul moves on in this passage to address the concept that there are varieties of gifts, but one Spirit. This is huge. Don't miss it. It's so easy for Christians to narrow the playing field the Holy Spirit operates in due to lack of knowledge and understanding Biblically. I am so thankful for those who know so much more than I do (admittedly that number is large). However, there is not one of them that understands it all, or all of any one part. We must not be fooled into thinking we've figured anything out in its entirety. Let's just look at this familiar passage again for good measure;

Isaiah 55:8-9 (NCV) 8 The Lord says, "My thoughts are not like your thoughts. Your ways are not like my ways. 9 Just as the heavens are higher than the earth, so are my ways higher than your ways and my thoughts higher than your thoughts.

Friends, this should not threaten you, but give you great comfort. What god would be worthy of serving and giving your life to that you could also have equality with? This is why Paul is stressing to the people of Corinth the Spirit is the One who makes all the gifts available, useful, and productive. This is why we, like they, must depend wholly on Him, and we must work together in harmony. This is necessary for God's methodology to work in your life and the life of all communities of believers.

Gifts don't come by trying hard or wanting them badly. They aren't taught or bought (although learning about them and growing in them is critical). What are spiritual gifts? A great place to start is in 1 Corinthians 12:8-10. Just being good at something or having an interest in something does not necessarily make it a spiritual gift. Spiritual gifts are not the same things as natural gifts, talents, and abilities. That being said, it doesn't mean that God can't and doesn't use them together to accomplish His will.

Here is a short list of gifts we see in Scripture (although not an exhaustive list): Wisdom, Knowledge, Faith, Healing, Miracles, Prophecy, Discernment, Various Tongues, Interpretation, Mercy, Hospitality, Giving, Administration, Teaching, Leadership, Exhortation, Shepherding, Evangelism, Apostleship, Service/Help, Encouragement.

Why do you have them and what's the point in using them? Once again, you can see this in 1 Corinthians 12:12-26. Spiritual Gifts are not for your benefit (as its primary purpose). We read that these gifts are for Stewardship & Service / Truth & Love / Unification & Strengthening / Health & Growth /

Helps us stay in our lanes and serve from the areas we are gifted (which are also roles and responsibilities).

1 Peter 4:10-11 is another great passage describing these grace gifts. The apostle Peter says that every believer has received grace gifts (plural). Staying in line with the chapter's theme of methodology, Peter makes it clear how these are to be used— to serve one another. Do you know why you were given these gifts? So that in everything God would be glorified through Jesus Christ.

What's Your Role? In 1 Corinthians 12:27-31 we're given this reminder that each of us has a unique and vital role in the church regarding our gifts. And we must put them into practice if the church is going to be healthy, whole and effective in all that God has intended it to be. In this text, Paul makes it clear that not any one person has all the gifts. Not all at once anyway. And, it is God who has appointed these roles and responsibilities within the church. Not a man. Let's explore the "practice" piece of this.

PRACTICE

Francis Chan's book *"Letters To The Church"* describes this notion that if we allowed God to prune His church down to those who really loved Him and obeyed Him, we might actually see some serious fruit. The alternative, according to Chan, is to continue letting the dead branches continue sucking the life out of the tree.[29]

It was not supposed to be complicated. Man has taken something simple and made it nearly impossible to function correctly. Anything God has given us must be Spirit-led for it to work correctly. The church is that very entity. When man attempts to run the church, it is devoid of the power of the Holy Spirit. God does not share His throne. Jesus will not give up His right as the Groom.

We were blessed to be exposed recently to this "Farm to Factory" concept. It connected with us deeply and personally. Our friend and local pastor, Destined Wright, shared one day with us this costly and tragic analogous shift in the Christian church. He compared these two different paradigms for ways

29   Can, Francis, *"Letters To The Church,"* Kindle location 853 of 2302, David C. Cook, Crazy Love Ministries, 2018.

of believing and living: 1) Farm 2) Factory.[30]

THE FARM

Back in the day, life revolved heavily on farming. School times were based on what happened on the farm. Working the farm took the whole family, and involved the entire community. Trade revolved heavily around farming. Employment was greatly affected by farming. Here's the thing about farming, when people put their hands to the plow (literally and figuratively), they would do all they could but had no control over two important things: the weather and the harvest. So, farming communities knew how to pray! They were grateful for what they had been given to sow but were utterly dependent on the Creator for what they would reap. Laziness had no place in this kind of society because it could lead to ruin and destruction. People needed God. People needed each other. Ultimately, people knew that God was in control of what they would have for survival and advancement. Prosperity in the home, local communities, church and the country as a whole looked very different then. Climbing the corporate ladder was not a concept or concern like it is today.

THE FACTORY

Factories have been around quite a while but were such the minority in American production and commerce. The first recognized factory dates back to 1790. It was a cotton spinner named Samuel Slater who built a factory to produce spindles of yarn. Fast forward to mainstream factories. Now you have fewer people with hands in the dirt and on the plow. We moved to people pushing a button and pulling levers to give us what we want. We can create things on our own and are far less dependent on nature, community, and God for the outcome, and even survival and advancement (so we think anyway). Add to that the increased level of competition, control, and independence. It's a whole new world.

Don't get us wrong; we are grateful for the advancement in technology, medicine, and the likes. The unfortunate side

30   Wright, Destined, adapted concept from dialogue, Pastor, Brentwood Neighborhood Church, Brentwood, CA, 2019.

effects have made their way into the community of believers and radically altered our connectedness and effectiveness as a family reaching the world together with the love of God.

This unfortunate shift has been a significant catalyst to another major modern-day shift. Too many have moved the advancement of the Gospel from one paradigm, "Go and Tell" to the less effective "Come and Hear." If we have any hope of seeing this corrected, we must be committed to a reframe where faith is practiced and rooted in the Word of God. We must return to a simpler faith and way of living, including our mission, vision, values and strategies/methodologies.

MISSION / VISION / VALUES / STRATEGY (MVVS)

If we don't understand the mission, we will have no clear or concise vision. This will cause conflicting values as well as convoluted and ineffective strategies. This is what led us to develop a simple system many years ago. There are a million of these out there, but this is just what the Lord gave us. We believe in this so much so that we have carried it with us to several churches, and taught in other venues.

Mission

Doing whatever it takes by all means necessary to bring the WAY, the TRUTH & the LIFE to all who are wayward, misled and dying.

Vision

As a church, we fulfill the mission by being a GATHERING, TRAINING, SENDING Hub.

Values

Our core values are all based upon and found in The Bible. Therefore, our governing values are LEARNING, LOVING, LIVING God's Word personally and together as the family of God— the church.

Strategy

Develop mentality, culture and eventually our DNA around living in missional community— a life on mission and a church on mission. A major step in this is comes when we connect with other entities within our community. It's also reflected in the way we teach and preach. It should drive the focus of the different groups and studies that eventually meet all over the community.

For a strategy to work, it requires trust. It is trusting God, trusting your leadership, and trusting each other. There are always those who want to do their own thing, and that in and of itself is not bad. However, learning how to connect what you're doing with your local church is even better. And, that requires a lot of prayer and fruit of the spirit (Galatians 5:22-23). What you are doing may be right, but the way it is intended to fit into the context of the local church is what makes it even better.

Luke 5:17-26 serves as a great example using this MVVS template.

FROM JESUS' VIEW [PERFECT EXAMPLE]:

Mission: FULFILLING HIS FATHER'S WILL

- Healing (physically and spiritually)
- Fulfilling God's plan of redemption for all of God's Creation

Vision: SETTING THE CAPTIVES FREE

- Seek the broken so they may be healed and in turn others may seek healing as well
- To see the good news reach the nations

Values: SURRENDER / OBEDIENCE

- Persistence, humility, of the broken
- Total surrender / Total obedience

Strategy: MEET THEM WHERE THEY ARE

- Live among the broken and love them in their current condition.
- Bring healing and hope so that it would be shared with others.
- Reveal His power through healing the mind, body and spirit so others would see Him as the Way, Truth and the Life.
- Meet the people where they are.
- Spend time with the lost and wayward. Heal and care for their needs to demonstrate the love of God.

This is an interesting setting here. Jesus is teaching to both the people and Pharisees. The Pharisees were really outside the realm of Jesus' mission but used them to show how the Jews had strayed from God's Mission. Seeing the faith of the friends who laid the lame man at his feet, and the faith of the lame man, Jesus heals him but does it in a way to accentuate His Mission. He equates the forgiveness of the man's sin with saving the lost, and in this case, healing the iniquities within the lame man. Jesus' Mission met both their physical, and more importantly, their spiritual needs!

FROM THE FRIEND'S VIEW [GOOD EXAMPLE]:

Mission: HURTNG FRIENDS HEALED
- Seeing hurting friends healed.
- To do whatever it takes with the means they had available to see if they could help their friend get well.

Vision: GETTING THEM TO THE HEALER
- Bring hurting friends to Jesus (short term mission).

- Each one identify and pursue hurting friends and take them to Jesus wherever He was.

Values: COMMUNITY / FRIENDSHIP
- Community, healing, responsibility

Strategy: WHATEVER IT TAKES
- Think outside the box
- Front door / back door / roof - Personally Carry their friend where he could not go himself.
- Show people the Way so they can experience the Truth & receive eternal Life.
- Figure out where Jesus was, figure out how to get the lame man in front of Jesus, ask Jesus for help.

There were plenty of obstacles, excuses and even legitimate reasons why it just wouldn't work. The friends of the lame man were faced with significant obstacles. First, people shunned the lame in those times. Secondly, there was no way to get through the crowd to Jesus— there was just no room. Thirdly, they had to figure out a new plan. They had to think way out of the box for them to accomplish what they set out to do (which was good and right). They could have thrown in the towel and perceived the obstacles as God's way of telling them it wasn't meant to be. Fourthly, they had to lift the man to the roof, no easy task with dead weight. Finally, they had to "dig" a hole in the roof to make an opening and had to figure out how to lower the lame man down rather than drop him. Whatever was necessary by whatever means available had to be invoked for them to succeed in their mission.

FROM THE RELIGIOUS LEADER'S VIEW [BAD EXAMPLE]:

Mission: PROTECT LAW & TRADITION
- To follow and obey their understanding of the

law of God and protect their traditions

Vision: RULE & REGULATE PERFECTION

- The law itself and all of its rules and regulations will keep unity and peace— Christ was not a part of their vision as He wasn't how they pictured Him to be.

- Advance themselves by being as perfect as they could with the law and practice, and to help others by making sure when they got it wrong it was corrected.

Values: TRADITION / ROUTINE / CONTROL

- Tradition, routine, control— Rules over relationships

- To love God by being an example of the kind of person God said they needed to be— Value being better than others by their superiority complex in holding fast to the customs and traditions.

Strategy: PUNISH THOSE LIVING OTB (outside the box)

- Shut down any new idea, keep everything the same, punish those who dared to think differently, kill those who would stand in the way of their vision and mission, use their knowledge to manipulate and deceive the masses to keep things under control, secret meetings to devise plans against those they feared, plan in secret in order to protect their position in public.

- Make sure no one or no thing came between their understanding of God and the rules.

- Be with the people to help them understand

the error of their ways and help them to follow Gods requirements as it fit their agendas.

The religious leaders immediately questioned Jesus about His statements because those statements did not match the religious leaders' understanding of God. They had no clue that Jesus was God. So when Jesus says He forgives sin, as a human, in their minds Jesus had blasphemed. Then, Jesus, as part of his mission to reach the heart of people for God, tells them what they are thinking and corrects them. The lame man being healed and God being glorified was the evidence of the correct MVVS.

The strategy is not what drove the lame man's friends. Purpose was. Hope was. Love was. Faith was. The strategy had to change as they met challenges along the way. And, they held to the mission and vision, with their values keeping them from giving up when it got difficult. The reason too many fail on mission and vision if they even have one, is their focus being too intense on the strategy (which is the "how"), that they forget the "why" and "what."

Jesus wanted to show Himself as the Way, Truth, and Life. The friends wanted to bring their friend to Him. The Pharisees wanted to govern the ways, the truth and the life (what it was and who could have it, and how they could get it). Could it be that far too many churches are still functioning in this broken paradigm today?

MATTERS OF METHODOLOGY

We want to encourage each of you NOT to believe the lie that has crept into our churches and ministries. Platforms and publicity can never replace or improve on personal witness and testimony (face to face). We are given a message of salvation, redemption, restoration, and hope. And, we are charged with being Christ's witnesses and responsible to take that message to the world (Acts 1:8). Whatever the process or procedure, let's work more diligently to include in our methodology a more intentional effort toward reaching those who have not yet believed or received this life-changing message!

For further study, here are some great reminders:
- James 1:27
- Luke 14:12-14
- 1 John 3:17

We hope this gets you more and more excited about the church and your part in it. Go back and read Ephesians 4. Look at the results of a body of Christ operating on a right foundation and with proper structure. Focus on verses 11-16. Maybe these words stuck out to you as well: Mature, Fullness, Developed, Strong, Sincere, Deeper.

Also, notice the promises associated with this structure. Maybe you're in a church like this, or your church is on it's way to operating like this and receiving the blessings and benefits. Praise God for that. If that is not your story, pray and ask God how you can step up and see that become a reality. All of this awaits you in your new reframe!

SECTION 4

LIVING THE REFRAMED LIFE

CHAPTER 13

CELEBRATE THE SEASONS

CONSIDERING IT PURE JOY!

IS THIS SEASON OVER YET?

Why do we work so hard to make things green when they're just going to turn brown again? Why plant a garden if a winter freeze can thwart your progress? Why spread seed and fertilizer when you know the snow is coming? Why do we love some seasons, but dislike others? Do we not see that they are all connected? Have you ever wondered; if we knew the value of the disliked seasons and the part it plays in our preferred season, would we embrace and experience them differently? What would your experiences during those seasons look like then?

Learning to embrace and enjoy the different seasons can radically change your ability to have a deeper more fulfilling partnership with Jesus. There is a joy to be had in each season. There is always something God wants to accomplish in us and through us in each of the seasons of life. Maybe you're like us, and you've learned to do more than endure each season, learning to celebrate the seasons as well as enjoying the bright light of hope in the midst of them all.

Like Paul, you too can find joy even in the suffering. James says it like this;

> *James 1:2-4 (AMP) Consider it nothing but joy, my brothers and sisters, whenever you fall into various trials. 3 Be assured that the testing of your faith [through experience] produces endurance [leading to spiritual maturity, and inner peace]. 4 And let endurance have its perfect result and do a thorough work, so that you may be perfect and completely developed [in your faith], lacking in nothing.*

SEASONS - LESSONS FROM A SEED

A seed is a fantastic creation. Its very purpose is to be changed and then produce an abundance of fruit for a lifetime. It begins small, humble, and dependent. A seed has no power whatsoever in and of itself. It must rely on the work of an unseen Hand using many external circumstances to bring out necessary changes to its very being to yield the most excellent fruit. The seed is at the mercy of its owner, the one who purchased it, the one who cares for it in all seasons, the one who knows its full potential. The tiny seed cannot begin to fathom its future purpose— it can only see itself today, in its current season, and must trust that everything it's being subjected to is serving to ensure it will fulfill the purpose foreseen by the seed's owner. The seed must believe there is a reason for each season.

A seed begins in the hand of a caring owner who then surrounds the helpless little seed in fertile soil. This is a joyous new season where the seed drinks deep from its new surroundings, drawing from the many nutrients all around it that begin to change the little seed into something new entirely. The owner all the while is working diligently above, watering the seed tirelessly, watching it carefully to keep it from harm. It is a season of comfort and joy as it remains warm and well fed at the hand of its owner.

It would be easy to desire this season forever, to be dependent and soaking in the goodness all around it. But if the seed remains a tiny seed, it will never see the real reason for its existence— bearing fruit. So here, the seed has a choice; to surrender, to die and be changed into something entirely new and fulfill its ultimate purpose under the guidance of its owner, or forever remain a seed, soaking from everything around it, but never seeing the beauty of growth.

Should the seed choose to be changed at the hand of its owner and surrender to a higher purpose, it now will become a new creation, not even resembling its prior form. It springs from the dark rich soil, now sprouting from the ground into the bright light of day. It is still well watered and cared for, but it now faces another element in its life— heat. The seed has never felt the warm rays beating down on its fragile form before. Some days the temperature is tolerable, and it appears to be bringing strength to its new form, causing it to grow steadily day by day. The sprout can see the good in the occasional discomfort of this necessary heat, and so it continues to surrender to the elements it's been placed in by its owner, knowing that it is helping the sprout get one day closer to its purpose. And in this beauty of spring, the sprout becomes a lovely thing to behold. The circumstances around it have brought about strength and grace to its form. It even produces fragrant flowers from its branches for all to see and enjoy.

What a fantastic season, this spring. Growth. Strength. Beauty. The now budding tree could choose to stay here forever in its glory, a sight to be honored and praised by others. However, if it does, the seed still will not see the real purpose for its very existence. And it will find that beauty doesn't last forever.

The once gentle and warming rays from the sun have now become intense. The heat is truly on. It's just plain hot. The summer winds have long since blown away the beauty of spring. The fragrant flowers have wilted and fallen to the scorched ground below. The heat seems impossible to bear. The tree's roots sink ever deeper into the rich soil from where it once begins, drawing strength from its riches to endure the extreme heat above. It finds itself in a parched state, daily drinking from the water from its owner's hand, who still stands near to see it through this trying season of summer.

As the relentless sun bears down more intensely each day, this creates a season of faith in the tree's life. It simply must trust that this searing heat is essential, and for the ultimate good, once again ensuring it will someday bring the tree to its real purpose in life— to bear fruit. And while the fragrant flowers are long gone, the tree begins to see the buds of something new. The steadfastness of the tree that has chosen to embrace its seasons and surrender to its many external circumstances is now finally seeing some reward! Its branches are now showing their first miraculous signs of fruit. The fruit is small and not at all ready for the harvest, but the perseverance of the tree has genuinely brought about change. It is beginning to see the purpose for its existence, even in this most undesirable season.

The tree continues to live the life it chose way back as a tiny seed— to surrender fully to its purpose, to draw deeply and daily from the riches of its roots and the water from the owners hand, and to watch as all the seasons do their work in the tree's life to bring about fruitfulness. It's now the harvest. The abundance of the fruit is amazing— it just keeps coming! The trees branches are heavy with the rewards for its life of surrender and faith in its owner. The owner takes great pride in the crop that the tree has yielded. The owner is pleased with the abundant fruit found on its branches.

However, not every branch has fruit on it. Perhaps the tree didn't drink quite deep enough from the rich soil and water that once fed it so well at the beginning. Maybe the scorching heat of summer left the tree dry and brittle in places. The owner lovingly removes those unnecessary and unfruitful parts of the tree so that the tree can remain healthy and strong and productive. While this pruning may hurt and cause the tree even to feel it's lost a part of itself that it once knew and loved, again the tree must trust in its owner, and that he will only do what is best for the tree so that it may continue to fulfill its ultimate purpose.

What a life it's been! Humble beginnings in the hand of a loving owner. Growth and fragrant beauty of spring. Summer and its unrelenting heat that produced an abundance of both faith and fruitfulness. The cooling breezes of the harvest season, where the tree gets to see its real purpose for living, to increase and give back to a loving, watchful owner.

It is here that a chill of winter begins. The tree has lost all its beauty, all its fruit, all its glory. The tree may feel rather useless for a season. Its branches are barren. The warm sun seems to have hidden its rays. The once warm breezes have now turned bitterly cold. The tree may ache for warmth and beauty of other seasons here. It may be difficult to understand why the tree must endure such stillness, such silence, such blustering winds of winter.

Why even exist with such ugly barren branches? What could its purpose possibly be? It is in this icy season of deafening silence that the tree must continue to do what it chose in the beginning— a life of surrender and faith in its owner.

The tree must believe that just as each prior season before, it served greatly to bring it to its full potential, so will this wintery season of rest. It must continue in faith each day, drawing deep from its roots from what sustained it from the start. It must not give up. It must believe that the warmth of spring will return someday. It must trust that as long as it continues to see the light of day that it does indeed have a purpose, and the owner has a plan. It must understand that life is more than just the beauty of spring, the heat of summer, and the joyful harvest of autumn.

There is winter. It makes the tree rest. It prepares it for the dark days ahead. It is dark. It is cold, and even bitter at times. It is quiet. It seems useless and may also feel ugly. But like the others, this season by its very nature will pass. So the tree must continue to surrender to the fullness of life and its seasons, knowing the owner still cares, is always watching, and won't ever leave it alone.

SOLOMON & SEASONS

What's your favorite season of the year? Why? What's your least favorite season of the year? Why? Did you ever feel like a season was never going to end? What if you were to think of life being made up of seasons? Can you think of your favorite season of life? How about the season you thought would never end, or still has not ended (i.e., terrible two's, teenage years, relationship with in-laws, sickness, disease, broken relationships, failure)?

You can't escape seasons. Every place in this world has seasons. Some places are not as dramatic, but they are still there. Why do we like some seasons of life, but not others? As followers of Jesus, shouldn't we assume that all seasons are part of His gift to us? Who tells the gift giver "thanks for part of the gift, but no thanks for the other ones?" Do you get to say "I don't like your gift? I don't think it fits all that well. Not sure that will line up with where I'm headed."

Is there anyone out there who understands? Does anyone get this whole time, seasons, living thing? Solomon did at some level. In Ecclesiastes 3 we can see that Solomon understood that collectively, all our decisions, activities, times, and seasons could be bound up and eventually be made into something beautiful— something beautiful called LIFE!

Wait a minute. Wasn't this the same guy that said everything is meaningless? Everything in and of itself is meaningless. If we live with the belief that all seasons are good in their time, we live in cooperation with God. Even in the most extreme situations, we can know and live life without the tainted and skewed perspective of it being meaningless. How? Because we live life by Him, from Him, and for Him. We live our lives embracing all the seasons. And, we do so with a heart of thanksgiving, worship, and with a spirit of obedience and trust.

Ecclesiastes 3:1-8 says there is a time for everything... EVERYTHING!

For everything, there is a season, and a time for every matter under heave— "matter" is better translated "willful acts"— which of course we are all individually accountable for. Solomon is saying there is a season (duration of time) for every activity.

Below is Solomon's list of what he perceived to be a pretty thorough explanation of those activities in the seasons of life. For every action, there is a time, and every time there is a season (duration).

A time to be born, and a time to die.

A time to plant, and a time to pluck up what is planted.

A time to kill, and a time to heal.

A time to break down, and a time to build up.

If all of life was just growth, it would kill itself- there have to be things that die in order for things to be born and live.

A time to weep, and a time to laugh.

A time to mourn, and a time to dance.

A time to cast away stones, and a time to gather stones together.

A time to embrace, and a time to refrain from embracing.

A time to seek, and a time to lose.

A time to keep, and a time to cast away.

A time to tear, and a time to sew.

A time to keep silence, and a time to speak.

A time to love, and a time to hate.

A time for war, and a time for peace.

We are fully aware of the sensitive nature and differing personal and political feelings and perspectives regarding war. We would ask that you always come back to Scripture when faced with any and all tensions regarding personal sensitivities to such issues. Once again, we operate with the understanding of our fallen world and carnal nature.

Consequently, we have seen war since Genesis. We have seen it done properly and justly (when God gave the commanding orders). And, we have seen it fail miserably (with man as the ultimate decision maker). Either way, there is a time for both.

Here is a perspective— A season is not life, it's a season within life. Those seasons will be filled with the good and the bad. The ups and the downs. But it can still be a full and abundant life. Jesus said that He came to give us life, abundantly— not good or bad, just life more abundantly. We associate abundance with "good." Maybe we need to stop qualifying life as hard or easy, good or bad, difficult or easy. These are overly exaggerated based on circumstances, likes and dislikes, feelings (again, too subjective). What about life makes us think there is a reality that exists where there is no difficulty, hardships, pain, suffering, struggle, failure, or weakness? Wouldn't life be unbalanced without that side of it? Would we look superior to Jesus? Do we now?

There is a reason for your season. There is a purpose and hope. God knows all your unmet dreams and desires. He knows all your successes and failures. Even the bird that falls out of the sky, He knows about it and is still in control. Remember, seasons are all under the ultimate authority of the Almighty God.

Seasons are never just about the here and now. And, it's never just about you— how you feel or what you think. It all fits into a much larger picture. Hence the reason for a reframe. The picture would not be complete without you and all your seasons. You may have to go through an undesirable season for you to experience a desirable one. You are a part of the bigger picture.

However, there will be things that happen to you that will add to the greater picture. Are you ok with that? Are you alright that there is not a "life" just for you? Serving and knowing God here and now is part of the reward. It is all part of this great gift called LIFE!

People get that discipline pays off and is ultimately worth it when it's something they love and want to succeed in. There is no other way to become better in those areas without sacrifice and discipline. If we believe this, then why would we not apply this to our spiritual development? Maybe we should shift the emphasis from praying for God to deliver people from their hardships and struggles to asking Him to reveal Himself to them through those experiences.

Seasons bring different things, that's why they're called seasons. They have functions, purposes, directives. All of them have benefits that you don't want to miss. Seasons take time (sowing):

- Noah building the ark... 120 years
- Abraham... 25 years (from God's promise of a son to the birth of his son)
- Joseph... time in prison and slavery
- Israel in slavery... 150 years
- Thomas Edison / Light Bulb
- Becoming a doctor
- Parenting / Grand-parenting
- Marriages
- Friendships
- Relationship with Jesus

Are you with us? Seasons, friends. It's bigger than you, but it's good for you. Embrace the season you're in and don't just endure them. They are from the Creator, and they are good! They are for your good and the greater good.

In Ecclesiastes 3:9-15 we see what we are to do with all of this. We keep living life in all of its seasons. We move and operate in our God-given tasks. We live with an ongoing sense of awe as well as an understanding and appreciation that eternity is real, and we are completely unaware of what's really going to happen tomorrow. However, this passage also makes it very clear that God is still in control of it all!

That's why we can move throughout our short time in this life, and see these seasons as necessary, beautiful, and given by the Creator God Himself. Let this passage really sink in;

Ecclesiastes 12-13 (ESV) 12 I perceived that there is nothing better for them than to be joyful and to do good as long as they live; 13 also that everyone should eat and drink and take pleasure in all his toil— this is God's gift to man.

God has given you the gift of life to be fulfilled and enjoyed. The duration of this life has not been made known to you. So you need to make the most of every season, every experience, every opportunity for as long as the Lord allows it to be called "today." How do you do that? We can think of no better way than to praise and worship Almighty God. Praise the Creator. Praise your Father in Heaven, your Savior, your Counselor (the Spirit of God). Do you want to see all this in perspective? Praise Him! This will be a reframe that changes your life!

REFRAMING YOUR SEASONS

Colossians 3:15-17 is a great passage of Scripture to rest in as you celebrate the seasons. Please read it as you can. Here are a few words of encouragement from the text:

- Jesus wants to guide you with His peace.
- So much of your peace is found in the context of the church body.
- There is a flood of wisdom waiting for you as you learn and apply His Word to your life.
- The Holy Spirit will bring words of worship to your heart, mind and lips- even spontaneously.
- Let all the words of your mouth, mediations of your heart and actions of your life bring ongoing praise to your Father in Heaven because of the beauty and wondrous works of your Savior, Jesus!

As you experience different seasons, what have you learned about trusting Him through them? What encouragement would you offer someone else who is experiencing an unfavorable series of circumstances in their current season?

CHAPTER 14

ALL IN

OUR ONLY RESPONSE!

ALL MEANS ALL!

We all struggle in some area of our lives when it comes to "All." There are too many believers that are still under the impression and illusion that when it comes to living a spirit-filled life, they can give anything less than their all. You are never kind of or mostly faithful. Faithfulness requires all of you— heart, soul, mind, and strength (Mark 12:28-31). God has given us His all. Our only response is to give Him our all.

There is a great parable about this very concept found in Matthew 25:14-30. It's called The Parable of the Talents. The parable is about a master who gives different amounts (talents) of his estate to his servants. Upon his return, he found that all but one invested with a return. Those who invested well were compensated accordingly. The other one did not invest, and was called a "wicked and slothful servant."

Yikes! Here are some of the concepts Jesus addresses in this parable:

It's the awareness of ownership.

It's the understanding of love.

It's the application of surrender.

In other words, it's all about a relationship. In this parable, they had all been given talents (resources). The number of resources that he gave was based on their abilities. This is a crucial point. What they would do with it is in direct correlation to what people, in general, do with it. That's why Jesus used parables like this— they speak to each of us and have real life-changing responsibilities and results. Let's journey a little deeper into this parable.

Take a look at The Giver as described in verses 14-15. First of all, you can't separate the Gift and the Giver. The Gift is always an extension of the Giver, and those Gifts are to be used for the glory of the Giver. Meaning, whatever the Giver does, the Gifts are for the furthering of that work. This emphasis needs to be understood right from the beginning. The focus is not the gifts/talents/resources/etc. It's all about the Giver and what He wishes to accomplish with them.

Now for The Investment described in verses 16-18. The first two servants put the master's money to work and made a profit. Profit is subjective though. Profit is based on the master's preference (since he owns it). Investing in the right way is critical to pleasing the master. The third servant buried it— hoarded it foolishly. This is the classic cause and effect— fear and foolishness.

He had the wrong idea of the master/giver. He didn't operate in a healthy reality. He feared the master and thought him to be hard, unkind, and without compassion. The fearful servant believed the master did not have the servant's best interests at heart. So, he reacted accordingly. His fear was for his provisions and profit. He wasn't convinced the master was even coming back. Best case scenario, if the master did not return, he could keep it all for himself. Worst case scenario, if the master came back he could give the bare minimum back to him (only that which was given to him).

Remember, all three of these are servants of the same master. All three had to do something with all of it. The first two invested it all! They kept none for themselves. Why? Because they knew none of it was theirs to keep. The third one kept it all. These are still your only options today. Why? Because all means all. The Master was not about to be impressed with a part and partial paradigm for living.

Finally, we can see The Results from each of these in verses 19-30. Make no mistake, there will always be results. The first two were rewarded for their faithfulness. They were given much more (to invest for the master). You may remember that the initial gift, as well as the "much more" was not theirs, to begin with. The greater reward was the master being willing to entrust his provisions to them because he knew they would use it to further the master's will— which is always the point. The enjoyment was getting to receive it and use it. Not receive it and keep it.

The results for the third servant was much different. The eye-opening experience for the third one was that he chose not to, at a bare minimum, put it in the bank so there would be interest. It was the master's interest on the master's money. The lack of faith in his master is what determined his worthlessness/uselessness (as opposed to good and faithful) as a servant. Faulty thinking leads to faulty living. The master's primary reason for his disapproval in the third servant was more about the wasted opportunity with what he had been given rather than the same amount being returned.

In this parable, the emphasis was all about the master (the owner of everything given to the servants). "What's best for the giver?" That's the right question. Not, "what's best for my family and me?" Why? Because it's all His. All of it. Not yours. His. Listen, your whole life changes the moment you understand this part of your reframe.

> John 3:27 (ESV) John answered, "A person cannot receive even one thing unless it is given him from heaven."

Did you know that Jesus talked as much about money as He

did any other subject (other than the Kingdom of God)? He didn't say "give me your money." His teachings were about the wisdom necessary for being good stewards and how to live this out. It's not about the money? That seems to be the one thing the Lord knew would be our hangup. Man, was He ever right! He knew this would be what kept us from giving Him our all. All means all. Not just what you think is yours (which we already know is an illusion and lie from the enemy). It's everything— all things. Time is not even yours. Breath is not even yours. Your body is not even yours. We are stewards. Please believe this truth— it will change your whole life. We promise!

Major "aha" moment of the parable is that you will always live your life based on the way you perceive the Father and His love for you. You will love in kind to the way you believe you are loved. Thus, you will live generously (surrendered) as you believe you have been given. The greater gift is being reconciled to God through Christ. We were forgiven, so we forgive. Sometimes, the problem is that we want to see an immediate return on our investment. Yet, many times what we give in this life isn't for us, but the next generation.

Remember, God is always more concerned about your relationship with Him than He is your environment, cultural context, and creature comforts. All the other things that He knows we need (by His standards, not ours) would be added. We simply need to live out this following statement;

> Matthew 6:33 (ESV) But seek first the kingdom of God and His righteousness, and all these things will be added to you.

This reminds us once again about that critical conversation between God and Solomon. What do you really want? Why?

The right questions lead to the ability to receive and apply the right answers. The right question is not "how much should I give?" It's not "how much do I have to give?" These are all questions someone would ask if they were first starting their faith. Even then, it would only be right to the degree they desire to know and do God's will. The reason those questions are not the right ones to start with is, it bypasses the most important question first— Do I remember that it's all His? And, am I stewarding (based on His preferences outlined for in Scripture) His resources according to His will? This is also an issue of love. Ultimately, this is THE issue. If we love Him, we love Him with all our heart, soul, mind and strength. All means all.

The Tithing / Offering Debate

- There is no "my money" and "God's 10 percent". It is all His, all for His use through you. The point is: Tithing is a discipline, just as your savings and retirement is a discipline. But tithing is a discipline of faith. Where is your faith? Do you trust God with His work through His people, the church? Do you believe that God has a work in the church at large different than any other place and space in life? If you do (and you should), then you also know this is an issue of obedience.

- 1 Chronicles 29— it's God's plan for the kingdom work to continue beyond our time here on earth.

- The New Testament did not make way for people to become selfish and not represent God's heart. The Father did not change just because Christ came (Malachi 3:6). Jesus coming only made this truth an even greater reason to be generous— above and beyond.

There is so much at stake here based on what you believe concerning this truth. Two compelling pieces of Scripture that deal with the heart and motive of giving are Matthew 23:23 and Mark 12:41-44. The emphasis in these two passages concerns matters of mercy, faithfulness, negligence, abundant giving, and a general mentality of giving your all.

God has given us opportunities to invest in people according to our abilities. How are we investing? Are we making the most of every opportunity as the Bible instructs us to do (Ephesians 5:16)? Are we choosing to store up for ourselves treasures on earth where moths, rust destroy and thieves break in and steal (Matthew 6:19-20)? Or, will we choose to store up treasure in heaven where those things do not affect (influence) or effect (the result of the influence)?

But it's still God's primary way of reaching the world (disaster relief & ongoing needs in our own backyard). Churches can reach individual families directly, person to person. If a church family isn't faithful in following God's call to give, then the church as a whole cannot provide for the people that need it most— the wayward, the misled and dying. Those that don't know Him and need Him desperately. Those far from Him. Those who've lost their way. And yet, this is no replacement for those divine opportunities to be generous to each other on a personal level, especially those in need.

> *1 John 3:17 (TLB) But if someone who is supposed to be a Christian has money enough to live well, and sees a brother in need, and won't help him— how can God's love be within him?*

Faithfulness and generosity are the model mindset for the way we live while our Master is "away." Jesus is coming back. We've staked everything on that fact as followers of Jesus. The rest of Matthew 25 is essential to consider. It finishes out Jesus' message about how we live in these last days before His return.

This notion of being given authority to rule over something is pretty incredible. We don't own it, but we have been entrusted with more to rule over because of our obedience with the lesser. To rule over still implies that we will rule within the boundaries of obedience, surrender, and all things according to His will and for His glory and benefit, not our own. However, we will always benefit, directly or indirectly. When the truth takes root, and it becomes more than a principle to argue, it can produce a crop of great abundance. That's why God can do much with little.

CAUTION / WARNING SIGN:

Matthew 13:22-23 (ESV) 22 As for what was sown among thorns, this is the one who hears the word, but the cares of the world and the deceitfulness of riches choke the word, and it proves unfruitful. 23 As for what was sown on good soil, this is the one who hears the word and understands it. He indeed bears fruit and yields, in one case a hundredfold, in another sixty, and in another thirty.

Luke 12:15 (ESV) And he said to them, "Take care, and be on your guard against all covetousness, for one's life does not consist in the abundance of his possessions."

1 Timothy 6:17-19 (ESV) 17 As for the rich in this present age, charge them not to be haughty, nor to set their hopes on the uncertainty of riches, but on God, who richly provides us with everything to enjoy. 18 They are to do good, to be rich in good works, to be generous and ready to share, 19 thus storing up treasure for themselves as a good foundation for the future, so that they may take hold of that which is truly life.

The Master is returning. And, there will be an accounting that will take place. You don't want to be deemed lazy or wicked. One day, when the Master returns, we too will be given much more. Much of that will be based on the level of surrender in this life now. Did He have your all here? Did He have your full surrender? If not, you can make that adjustment here and now. Once that happens, you will be living with the mindset and under a new reality that all means all— He is and has your all!

This whole thing called life, and all that goes with it is not about promoting personal interests, pleasures, and desires. If that's a person's hangup, then they might as well keep doing what they're doing. Keep living for themselves. Here's the harsh reality with that, whatever a person gets on their own will be all they'll have. They may think they're satisfied, but it's because they haven't seen the other side yet. If they knew, they would never be the same, and they would never knowingly want to go back.

Here's another thought— your love and loyalty determine attitude and actions. Everything we've talked about in this chapter is ultimately about a relationship. Ownership, stewardship, faithfulness, giving, sharing, loving, investing... it's all about a relationship. So, why in the world would anyone let what was intended for deeper dependency on Christ be the wedge that divides and separates? Love compels us. So the question is, if you're not compelled, why?

We can only be as obedient, effective, useful together as we are individually. The "church" can do no more than its members. People say all the time that "the church" needs to _____. But again, we cannot do collectively what we do not do individually. Our strength and effectiveness lie within our individual members of the body all working together as the Bible instructs.

> *1 Corinthians 12:18-20 (ESV) 18 But as it is, God arranged the members in the body, each one of them, as he chose. 19 If all were a single member, where would the body be? 20 As it is, there are many parts, yet one body.*

Jesus tells us in Luke 6:38 that we are to give. The result is, it will be given to us. That's actually how we have it to give. The giving starts with the heart (obedience and faith), and He will supply what we need to actually do the giving (or He has already given it and wants you to now give accordingly). He even goes as far as to say the measure we give is the measure we will receive. So, why would anyone ever want to give little, knowing that the same standard of giving will be used in returning to them? Why would they doubt this truth?

Make no mistake, there are consequences for doubting. It's not as much punishment as it is the repercussion of not taking God at His Word. Here are some examples:

Gideon doubted his strength to lead in Judges 6 and 7, saying he was the least of the least. God stripped down his army to 300 men to prove that victory was not about man's strength at all.

James tell us in James 1:5-7 that we are double-minded and unstable in our minds if we ask for wisdom in Jesus' name, but doubt He will respond accordingly.

Moses doubted his ability to speak in Exodus 4. So, God made a way through Aaron.

In the books Exodus, Leviticus, Numbers and Deuteronomy, we see how the Israelites doubted God's ability to deliver and lead them, and it cost them an entire generation as God waited for their doubt to die.

In Genesis 16, Abraham and Sarah doubted their bodies could produce a child. They made their own plan through Hagar and had Ishmael. God made them wait 13 more years for their promised son, Isaac. Isaac and Ishmael (their descendants) are still at war to this day in the Middle East.

In John 20, Thomas doubted the resurrection and needed proof. Jesus questioned his need to see first before having faith, and said blessed are those who believe yet have not seen.

Do you trust God? He is the Author and Giver of life. He is the Sustainer and Provider. Do you trust Jesus? He is the Prince of Peace and the Hope of Salvation. Do you trust the Holy Spirit? He is the One that will empower and enable you to hear, see, and do what you cannot in your own strength and will.

Will you love the Lord your God with all your heart, soul mind and strength? Because that's the "all" He is after. It's His greatest command because it's His greatest way to give you His greatest gifts.

FISH OR CUT BAIT

Have you have heard the expression "Fish or cut bait" before? The message is simple, make a decision. This sometimes is an issue of confidence. If you're honest, what areas of your life and faith do you struggle trusting God in?

Remembering the faithfulness of God is always a huge help in overcoming the fear of trusting God with your all. Look back at your life (as well as history in general). Start by thanking and praising God for His faithfulness, even if it 'didn't turn out the way you had hoped.

Lastly, what do you need to release and walk away from to be all in? Start with one of them, trust God with it, and see how He will bless you. He does love you. He is all in with you. Will you be all in with Him?

LET US LEAVE YOU WITH ONE LAST THOUGHT:

Whatever you think is currently providing for you is the very person or thing that you will seek to please and praise.

CHAPTER 15

SECRET TO SUCCESS

THE VICTORY IS YOURS!

SUCCESS

What is the secret to success? It depends— at what do you want to be successful? If you're going to be a professional athlete, then just reading a lot of books on the subject may not bring the greatest success. You would need to get out on the field, court, ice or wherever and play. You need coaching. You need to learn the fundamentals and disciplines of the sport. Then, whatever the standards and principles are for that sport that determines success, you have to accomplish the objective.

One of the greatest struggles you face in this time, place and space is the conflicting messages, definitions, and examples of success. What is a success? Who is successful? How do you know? What if you're wrong? What will you do to get it? Be it? Have it? How do I look and act the part? Where will it take me?

Answering the question concerning success is critical in understanding how to live that way. Who gets to define success? According to leadership expert Stacia Pierce, it looks like this:

> "In a business setting, your appearance matters. Your image educates others on how you want to be approached. Every time you go out, you reflect an image that tells others how to treat you. They are sizing you up and making an assumption of what you do for a living, your income level and your current level of success in life based solely on your appearance."[31]

There are many parallels here— from the inside and out.

SUCCESS:

the accomplishment of an aim or purpose;

the attainment of popularity or profit.

How shall we define success?

For the third-world country… it's survival

For the struggling student… it's passing

For the terminally ill… it's healing

Part of our problem is that we do not start with the end in mind. If we told you that you could choose between living in a small house now, or be homeless, you'd probably want the house. But, what if I told you the rest of the story? If you would remain homeless for one more month, you could have a mansion in the greatest spot you could imagine, and it would be ready for move-in? In other words, your home is not ready, and you need to forgo some pleasure and conveniences as well as endure some uncomfortable situations. Can you do it? You'd probably wait as long as it took and not think it was much of a sacrifice, especially when the gain would be greater than what you were temporarily giving up. This temporary

31   Pierce, Stacia, "*What Does It Mean to Dress for Success?*," www.huffpost.com, November, 2014, retrieved May, 2016, https://www.huffpost.com/entry/what-does-it-mean-to-dres_b_5875952.

discomfort is actually part of the success.

Success can be seen in Colossians 3:1-17. This is Paul's letter to the churches in Colosse addressing how to live as victorious Christians. He tells them to set their minds on things above, and not on earthly things. He tells them to put to death anything that belonged to their former way of living (before knowing Christ). Then, he tells them to clothe themselves with characteristics of Christ— compassion, kindness, humility, gentleness, and patience. Since they are God's chosen people and dearly loved, Paul tells them how to treat each other within that love. Ultimately, in this passage, Paul tells them to let the peace of Christ rule in their hearts. This would be evidence of them all being members of one body. That's what it looks like to be dressed for success.

Notice the two main action points in dressing for success that Paul addresses. The first one was to take off some things (The Old Self). The main reason you take it off is that it doesn't fit you anymore. You have outgrown them. Otherwise, it's the more mature and wiser wanting to look and act like the younger and less wise. Here are those old things our Old Self represents that we were told to remove:

Sexual Immorality/ Impurity/ Passion/ Evil Desire/ Covetousness/ Idolatry/ Anger/ Wrath/ Malice/ Slander/ Obscene Talk/ Lying

Those were items of success for the envious, jealous, proud, arrogant, unhappy and dissatisfied. Conversely, he tells us to put some things on.

Paul says, "Hey, you can't be naked, so put these on. They'll fit perfectly" (The New Self). This is what represents who you are in Christ. It sets you apart. When you wear these things, people can tell much easier who you are and what you live for. These represent your New Self:

Compassion/ Kindness/ Humility/ Meekness/ Patience/ Forbearance/ Forgiving/ Love/ Peace/ Thankfulness/ Faithful in the Word/ Teaching & Admonishing

Those were items of success for the sold-out committed follower of Jesus— the secure in Christ (identity). This was the genuine Great Commandment and Great Commission-minded community.

Are you dressed as a consumer or investor? Another way to see it is, are you dressed as a fisherman & farmer, or a religious VIP factory worker? This kind of mindset does just enough to be considered spiritual but adopts a sense of being pretty important. So, investing in the ministry and life of the local church doesn't quite fit that life and lifestyle.

What does your life look like? What are you living for? Are you giving yourself away like the end is near? Are you spending the majority of what you have on yourself? Is your life tied up in you? What are we teaching the younger generations? What are we demonstrating to the world? Sometimes Christians live like they're in competition to look like the rest of the world, not set apart (which is the true identity of a follower of Christ).

Our personal story in this area is, our kids knew growing up that we chose to follow God in a way that meant we were not always going to have the same things that their friends had. We wouldn't always get to go to the same places their families got to go. And, we certainly weren't going to be at the same level socially that others would be. We were never going to be VIP's in this world. It's just not what God called us to be, or anything we would strive to be. We were probably never going to look like the culture's definition of "success." But that was good enough for us because we were not using the world's definition anyway.

So, you can see why defining success is key to knowing how to dress for it. This is your first step in really understanding how to be most effective in the Kingdom of God. The rest of Colossians 3 is what happens in our lives and homes when we get this right. You know, we want to partner with Paul here in reminding the reader what your driver and motivation should be.

Colossians 3:23 (TPT) Put your heart and soul into every activity you do, as though you are doing it for the Lord Himself and not merely for others.

DON'T DETACH!

Staying connected (Abiding) is the success in and of itself. All other success comes through you, not from you. There you go. You can stop there, or go ahead read the rest of this chapter.

You know, since we wrote it and all. Thanks.

Abide. The Greek word is *Meno*. It means continuing in; remaining in. Abiding in Christ is continuing and remaining connected to Him and His church. This is such an overlooked command packed with promises from God. Our work here on earth is curiously, dangerously, scandalously simple. We must abide. We must stay connected to, and rest in, the Vine.

We have to stop struggling against the Vine, trying to live apart from the Vine— apart from Jesus we can do nothing (John 15:5). Will we simply rest on our laurels? This is extremely dangerous and damaging to spiritual growth and causes uselessness in regards to Kingdom work.

So, if everything we receive comes from heaven (John 3:27), and if we are only fruitful due to our relationship with Jesus, abiding in the Vine, why would we ever feel the need to strive in this life? Why would we ever look anywhere else but to Jesus? You know, the One who assures us that fruit will appear as we abide? We are promised, even assured, that the outcome of our time and effort will result in nothing apart from our abiding relationship with Jesus. And, apart from Him, we can receive nothing. So, if we gain nothing, then my friends, we will have nothing to give.

The secrets of a fruitful life are all wound throughout our life in the Vine— abiding in the love of God, obeying His ways, and loving others. The vine handles the fruit production. All the goodness and ability and power flows from the Vine. Everything originates in and from the Lord, which then flows into us as connected, abiding branches. Abiding is the only activity given in the Word that is tied directly to the promise of fruit.

Abiding is simply a branch living in daily surrender to the ways and the work of the Vine. A branch is not to struggle against the vine, but to accept what flows through it, and to remain as closely connected as possible to ensure the timely arrival of abundant, healthy fruit. Abiding is surrender.

We must surrender to the still and quiet winter seasons, where unhealthy and unproductive parts that restrict the life-giving flow of the Vine are lovingly removed to strengthen and fortify the branch. We must surrender to spring, where there are buds with the hope of a bountiful harvest to come. Although it hasn't yet arrived, it will continue teaching us patience and trust. We must surrender to the heat and heaviness of harvest when the branch is weighed down with the abundance of fruit waiting to be shared with the world.

We must learn quiet surrender in every season, remaining steadfast in our connection and accept what comes from the Vine. We cannot allow ourselves that longing for one particular season to last the whole year. To ask this is to ask for the weakness of the branch. The return is always useless and poor quality fruit. Abiding in the Vine is a life of connection to our Source and surrender to each season. Submission alone will bring a sure harvest and steadfast faith.

So the question remains: will we choose to steadfastly remain connected to the vine, even when we can't see a single spring bud or the tiniest of green leaves? Will we continue to trust the work of the Vine and the Vine Dresser in all seasons? The greatest challenge before us as branches is to believe that the purposeful, powerful work of the vine is present and active in every season we face. When you feel like bailing, don't! Don't run from your development.

Maybe ask yourself "What is God trying to teach me through this?" It makes us think of the old adage from Robert Frost, *"The best way out is always through."*

VICTORY OR VANITY

Everything we do in life as followers of Jesus Christ can fall into two categories: victory or vanity. Real victory and success comes when we abide. We just covered that. But take a close look at your life. If you've made it this far in the book, prayerfully you are getting more and more jazzed about beginning or continuing to think through what a reframe would like in your life. You have two choices according to Psalm 127; a life of victory or one of vanity.

> Victory: an act of defeating an enemy or opponent in battle.
>
> Vanity: excessive pride in or admiration of one's own appearance or achievements.
>
> Vain: producing no results, having no fulfillment or meaning.

Here's the catch. All of us are capable of vanity. Apart from Christ, it is all we are capable of. If you think otherwise, you pretty much just proved the point. Ha! Victory over the enemy seems doable in the flesh if you believe the enemy is a person, a place, and ideology or way of life. However, what does the Bible say about our enemy?

> *Ephesians 6:12 (ESV) For we do not wrestle against flesh and blood, but against the rulers, against the authorities, against the cosmic powers over this present darkness, against the spiritual forces of evil in the heavenly places.*

Can you see why the majority of Christians live so defeated, frustrated, depressed, and distracted? All the attempts, efforts and energies are too often done in vain. This only yields empty and frustrating results, lack of purpose and meaning, and a depressing lack of fulfillment. Psalm 127 tells us that unless the Lord builds the house and watches over the city, man labors in vain. If the Lord does not provide, man still labors in vain. Let's break it down.

Unless the Lord builds the house,
those who build it labor in vain.

Building a house for yourself or even for the Lord in your efforts will always be insufficient and lacking. Making a life for yourself or the Lord renders you the same. Proverbs 16:9 reminds us that we can plan our course, but success lies in the steps that have been established by the Lord. Proverbs 19:21 also speaks to this— man's best-laid plans can't compare to the prevailing purposes of the Lord.

Unless the Lord watches over the city,
the watchman stays awake in vain.

Try as we may, we cannot protect ourselves in our own strength and efforts. Trying to patrol or control your own life and family is futile. All the fires, storms, attacks, accidents and breakdowns will come. Even if you could stay awake every second, 24-7, it would still be in vain. You would be doomed.

Unless the Lord provides,
working hard for sustenance is in vain.

No matter how hard you work, how long you work, how much you earn, how much you give, how much you save or how much you gain and save. It's never enough. All this produces is exhaustion, lack of comfort and peace, then ultimately bitterness and disappointment.

One example of victory that was epic and critical for survival and the continuation of entire people groups is here in verses 3-5. Children were carrying out the family name. It was a sign of health and prosperity. It was critical protection for the family. God's favor and blessing. This is what He desires— favor and blessing in and through your life. Victory in life, not vanity. Living in a way that brings life, a whole life, a fulfilled life. Living in a way that fills the void and emptiness from that ego-centric way of life we're so familiar with.

So, will we trust the Lord? His will? His plan? His timing? His resources? His way? Living in vanity is living in vain. Living obediently is the only way to live in victory. It's the only way to success. So, where do you start?

THE SECRET TO SUCCESS

Read Psalm 37:3-7. Take note of the different verbs that describe intimacy as the key to success (i.e., trust, do well, delight, etc.). Which of these are you experiencing joy in? Which of these are keeping you from walking in the success God has praised you? Pray and ask the Holy Spirit to show you the power that you possess in Jesus's name to receive, believe, and live out of the righteousness He has made real in you.

In the midst of it all, don't forget the instruction given here;

> *Psalm 37:7 (ESV) Be still before the LORD and wait patiently for Him; fret not yourself over the one who prospers in his way, over the man who carries out evil devices!*

His provisions are based on His promises, purpose, and plans. Those are unlimited from Him. However, don't limit His provisions and promises to your plans. The degree to which you experience God's purpose, plans, and promise is dependent on Him being your source and provision.

We are painfully aware of the ongoing tension we must battle within our flesh. We want to do way more through God (believing He wants that too) than we believe He wants to do through us. The secret to success is simple. Don't let the enemy deceive you into thinking otherwise! You can do this!

Remember, only by abiding/remaining in intimate connection with Jesus (as The Vine), are we able to experience (as the branch). For further study, check out the following truths and their corresponding Scripture references:

the **FRUIT** of the Holy Spirit (Galatians 5:22-23)

the **POWER** of the Holy Spirit (Acts 1:8)

the **PEACE** of the Holy Spirit (Romans 15:13)

the **GUIDANCE** of the Holy Spirit (John 16:13)

the **GIFTS** of the Holy Spirit (1 Corinthians 12, 14)

CHAPTER 16

NEW, NEXT OR NOTHING

PUTTING REFRAME INTO ACTION!

RESPONSE REQUIRED!

Thank you so much for taking some time to join us on this journey of the reframed life. Jesus stepped right into the middle of our brokenness and brought healing and wholeness to our home, our relationships and most importantly, brought us to His feet. We look forward to all He has planned for us in the days ahead. But you know what? We're even more excited to think of all He has for each and every one of you! Your reframe!

The future holds such great and beautiful promises for God's kids. In fact, sometimes it's easy to get caught up in seeking what's coming up next rather than enjoy what's right in front of us. Sometimes we get into meteorologist mode and start forecasting what we believe our lives should look like using common sense and personal preference. But if there is anything we've learned on this journey, it's that God's ways are truly so much higher than our ways. His thoughts are so much higher than our own. We see so dimly here, friends. As such, our future forecasts are bound to be anemic and nearsighted without the infinite insight that belongs solely to our Creator and King. So, we must stop the forecasting.

FORECASTING

This is what we have to stop doing to ourselves. A proper reframe of our future allows us to live in victory here and now. He says that He knows the plans He has for us. They're His plans for us. We are not left to develop our own strategies for our lives and the Kingdom. If we persist in this, we will continue to establish fads, movements, revolutions and other "come and go" ways of living.

By nature, we will prepare for what we forecast. If there is rain, we will grab an umbrella. If there is snow, we grab a coat, scarf, and gloves. We will gear up for that which is in our future. If our internal forecast is wrong, we will be ill-prepared for the elements or season into which God is bringing us. If we gear up for conversations that we have already forecast to go awry, we will bring our defensive armor and be ready to strike at the first hint of a perceived attack. If we prepare our gardens for winter by cutting them back and covering them and it is spring outside, the garden will fail from lack of sunshine and water— from lack of what was needed in due season.

So when we read Ephesians 2:10 and it tells us we are His poetry and we were created in Christ Jesus for good works that God prepared beforehand, before our existence, we need to believe and honor that forecast. When we read that God has plans to prosper us, ultimately for His glory, we need to believe that forecast. Too often we are listening to the wrong meteorologist. We prefer to listen to the One who created the atmosphere and knows it best.

NEW. NEXT. NOTHING.

We have found over the years that there is a proper perspective on time that is often missing and in need of a reframe. We see it not just in Chronos (actual time) but in Kairos (window of opportunity within Chronos; appointed time or opportune time). God is doing something new, friends. This statement makes some of you uncomfortable. You might be thinking "Are you saying that God is doing something new that is not in the Bible?" Well, yes and no. Let's take a closer look before you throw the book down and yell "Heresy!"

In Isaiah, we're told not to remember the former things of old because God is doing a new thing and beautiful things will come from it.

> In 2 Corinthians Paul tells us that if we are in Christ, we are a new creation. The old is gone, and the new has come.

> In Ezekiel God promised to give them a new heart and a new spirit, and new things would be birthed from that.

God loves doing new things. He loves the word "new!" All of God's promises are fulfilled in Jesus. But all the works and wonders that Jesus did then and will continue to do among us now are not contained in the written Bible we have now. Still squirmy? What we're saying is, not all things that God is doing is recorded in the Bible. However, nothing new will ever conflict, compete, or contradict what is given us in His written Word. All of His acts were not, and could not, be recorded in a trillion books, much less one Bible. All of His miracles didn't make it. And, so much of what He has been doing since isn't in the written pages of our Bibles. However, if they are from the Lord, then they will be echoes of what is already there.

All truth and revelation are wrapped up in the person of Jesus Christ. So, whatever new word, revelation, or action is given to believers, it will always come back to Jesus. And, those words, revelations, and actions will always find their roots in the Bible. The argument really should not be on new, but whether or not it is consistent with the rest of God's Word.

NEW

Are you ready to move into something new? A new season submitted to the Spirit of God? A season of right alignment with His Word? A word of caution to you, friends: Don't settle for a repaired version of what you had in the past. God wants to restore you to the right version of you (perfect and complete in Christ— lacking in nothing). Not a repaired, retro-version of you. Culture is going to want to define you so that you're understandable to others or themselves. God has already defined you. The conflict between these two is what drives new, next or nothing.

Why are so many so threatened by the reality of new? It's not like it's new to God. Therefore, there is no need for concern that your theology would need to make room for that kind of instability in the sovereignty of God (Malachi 3:6/ Isaiah 41:4/Hebrews 13:8/James 1:17/Isaiah 40). But make no mistake, what we have recorded in the Holy Scriptures is not all there was, is and is to come. It's just all that we need to know for salvation, surrender, and sanctification.

It may be time to get out of the box that you have found yourself trapped in. Here's the deal though, be careful not to get out of one to jump into another one. A new box is not the "new" that we should be looking for. And don't get out of your box to get into someone else's box. This is equally defeating, frustrating and fruitless. Run your race, and you can succeed. You can never run another person's race. It was never for you. Therefore you can never win in it.

NEXT

So we know the definition of insanity: doing the same thing over and over and expecting a different result. Well, this is the word of caution for those consistently searching for what's next? Next may sound exciting and new, but in truth, our "next" may end up as a rearrangement of the old (practices and traditions). We may be longing for change, searching for the next assignment, next adventure, next endeavor, but in the end, we just repeat the same exploits in different clothes, with different people, and give it a different label. We're renovating the inside of the box. We're entering into extreme home makeover mode, where we may slap on some new paint, buy some new dishes and a throw rug, and suddenly we're on to the next phase of our lives.

The problem is we are still functioning in the same box. The walls haven't changed. The neighborhood hasn't changed. The routine hasn't changed. It's just prettier and more comfortable. It meets every standard for keeping up with the Joneses. We're staying in step with the next trend, the next big thing, the next worship trends, the next mid-week bible study. Next. Next. Next.

The problem with chasing what's next is that it doesn't leave room for what's new. It keeps us on the same hamster wheel, burning the candle at both ends, leaving us busy, tired, and empty. You see, there will always be the next thing. When we are motivated by what's next, it eats away at our contentment and drives us into the arms of comparison. Next keeps us in an unconscious state of competition with those around us, as we are always checking over our shoulder to see who got to the next thing first.

When we think about what's next, we strive to arrange, manipulate, figure out and plan/prepare for it. Next is just building more layers on the same old structure.

Ah, but when we think about what's new, that requires a much different type of trust and faith. It is for many a paradigm shift. A brand new reframe. At the least, it's a new level of discovering and living out our inner transformation. This process of sanctification becomes much more transparent and really exciting (and maybe a little scary).

When we surrender to the spring of living water within us, we have a new life, new hope, new insight, new clarity and new peace given graciously through the Holy Spirit within us. So don't let the shackles of needing what's next bind you from desiring what's new.

NOTHING

When faced with a fresh new insight revealed from God's Word, we have no choice but to respond. We can surrender to the new life in Christ, or choose to stay safe and wait and see what's next. Sadly, we can also choose to do absolutely nothing. That's right, nothing. We can choose to keep our feet planted firmly right where they are and keep living the life we've always known.

This, unfortunately, traps so many Christians, preventing them from experiencing the full work of Christ in their lives. Too many are missing out on the incredible and powerful work of the Holy Spirit in and through them. This was a part of our story for far too long. However, a proper reframe allowed us to be better equipped and more victorious in the battle over the vortex of nothing. The enemy does some of his finest work there. Look a little more closely at the deception and deceitful work of the enemy. Let's turn the light on his dark deeds that keep us trapped in lacking mode.

What leads to our lacking? Fear and doubt. Remember, it's one of the greatest tools (arguably his greatest weapon against followers of Christ). In Matthew chapters 7 and 8, we see what happens when Jesus enters the atmosphere— the response is either fear or faith.

We see some were drawn to Jesus and brought all the sick to him for healing, fully assured he would change them for the better. We also see that others saw his great power to drive out demons from the town outcasts, and the people begged Him to leave them (Matthew 8). The power and authority over the demonic frightened them. So we can gather that where the demonic is at work, it will manifest in fear.

Adam and Eve— they were under the influence of the serpent and it created fear. First, the fear of missing out, which led to fear of intimacy with God and led them into hiding.

The demonic was at work in the Gadarenes, a territory Jesus had just chosen to cross over stormy seas to get to, and they begged him to leave them after seeing His healing power.

Sarah feared her season of childbearing was officially over, and so fear of missing God's promise chose her to drum up "Plan B" for creating the promised child.

In the parable of the talents, we see fear driving a servant to hide his talent and await his master's return. He stated he believed his master to be a hard man, and so he didn't want to take a risk and mess anything up, so he just took the master's gift of talent and hid it in the dirt. That way it would be returned safely, and he would remain protected from his master's anger or disappointment.

When fear causes us to draw away from our Master, to hide in the trees, to bury our gifts, we are submitting to the leadership of the demonic. Our enemy wants to wedge his way into our intimacy with the Father. He's learned the most effective wedge is fear. Fear taps into our fleshly nature and stirs up the fight or flight reaction in our body.

When we submit to fear we will either fight against God or catch the next flight out to get away from Him. And, we won't really even have to think about it. God created fight or flight to keep us safe here on earth. It's our natural defense system. This is just like the enemy, right? He takes what God created as a beautiful, life-giving gift, and twists it to use against the Creator.

Perfect love casts out fear— fear of anything but the Lord, that is. When we walk in the Spirit, we have a healthy fear of the Lord because we have a healthy love for and with Him. When we are walking in the flesh, we have an unhealthy fear of and love for man. This in return causes an unhealthy fear and love with the Lord, as well.

So, when we read in the Bible that we are not to fear (Isaiah 41:10, 2 Timothy 1:7, 1 John 4:18), it has more to do with fearing anything other than God Himself. Psalm 23 says we will fear no evil. Proverbs 29:25 speaks to the snares of fearing man. Joshua 1 speaks to this same kind of fear. Psalm 27:1 asks the question "whom shall I fear?" Meaning, what mortal man should I fear?

Our only weapon against fear is faith. It's the only other option. We either trust God in His goodness, His sovereignty, His wisdom, and His Words— or we don't. When we don't choose trust, we submit to fear by default. We then become much more susceptible to the influence of the demonic and the enemy's schemes to drive wedge after wedge of fear between the Father and us. This strategy worked in the garden with the first two people in creation.

We are no different today. Fear or faith? Two masters. We can only serve one. Who do you choose to serve? You will make a choice intentionally or unintentionally. Either way, you are making the choice today. Our hope and prayer is for you to choose as Joshua did here,

Joshua 23:14-15 (ESV) 14 Now therefore fear the Lord and serve him in sincerity and in faithfulness. Put away the gods that your fathers served beyond the River and in Egypt, and serve the Lord. 15 And if it is evil in your eyes to serve the Lord, choose this day whom you will serve, whether the gods your fathers served in the region beyond the River, or the gods of the Amorites in whose land you dwell. But as for me and my house, we will serve the Lord.

YOUR REFRAME BEGINS NOW!

New, next or nothing? The choice is yours. Whether you make an active choice to step into the adventure of the new, or continue to strive in self effort with what's next, or make the passive choice to change nothing at all— you WILL make a choice.

So, friends, we ask you; What Do You Want? Is there a realignment in your decision today? Are you ready to be All In? Are you ready to join us in the reframed life? We pray the Holy Spirit has spoken to you through the many musings of our journey into faith and freedom. It's never too late to surrender to all God has stored up for you!

Live out your freedom! This is the joy of your salvation, and the reason for you to experience your own reframe!

Remember these truths:

Galatians 5:1 (TPT) Let me be clear, the Anointed One has set us free—not partially, but completely and wonderfully free! We must always cherish this truth and stubbornly refuse to go back into the bondage of our past.

John 8:36 (AMP) So if the Son makes you free, then you are unquestionably free.

2 Corinthians 3:17 (ESV) Now the Lord is the Spirit, and where the Spirit of the Lord is, there is freedom.

For further study, the Bible is full of examples of God's heart for newness:

Isaiah 43:18-19 / Isaiah 42:19 / 2 Corinthians 5:17 / Isaiah 42:10 / Ezekiel 36:26-29 / Revelation

2:17 / Revelation 21:3-8 / Revelation 1:1-20 / Lamentations 3:21-24 / Amos 3:7 / Ephesians 4:22-24 / Ecclesiastes 3:11 / Colossians 3:9-10 / Romans 12:2 / Psalm 65:11 / Proverbs 16:9 / add your favorites here…

APPENDIX

LAST THOUGHTS...

THE PRISON

One of the most important things you can be reminded of every day is the truth in this passage:

> *Galatians 51:1 (NCV) We have freedom now, because Christ made us free. So stand strong. Do not change and go back into the slavery of the law.*

You are no longer a slave to your own efforts. Your humanity and flesh are incapable of doing what Jesus already accomplished on the cross. The only way a reframe is useful is to remember that you have been set free, and you must now walk in your freedom. Freedom! You are free from guilt and shame. You are free to walk with God. You are free to love Jesus with all your heart, soul, mind and strength. You are free to grow in knowledge, wisdom, and discernment, thanks to the work of the Holy Spirit in and through you.

This freedom allows you to love, forgive, bear fruit and stay connected to the local body of believers (since you're a member of the Body of Christ). All of these things (and more) are made possible when you walk in relationship with Jesus.

A life of surrender is a life of freedom. A life of dependency on the supernatural power of the Holy Spirit is a life of freedom. This freedom also allows, and even compels us, to live out the Great Commission.

THE POOL

The pool analogy represents a healthy model for discipleship and relationships with others. Reaching people with the good news of the Gospel is more than just salvation. It's also about the process of sanctification and the pursuit of righteousness.

The goal of this analogy is three-fold. First, the church (the body of Christ) needs to be accessible at all levels of maturity, interest, and commitment. Some will enter from the shallow end, others through the side, and others through the deep end. You can draw your own parallels and conclusions as to what those entry points mean.

Secondly, deep water Christians (those who are more mature in their faith and the knowledge of God's Word) were never called to build their own community in the deep end. The Great Commission in Matthew 28 was not given for the apostles to form their own organization or church. They were called to go and make disciples all over the world. This can not happen apart from relationships with those who are in the shallow end. And, if you are at an early stage in your spiritual journey, you need those who have gone into deeper water ahead of you. Deep end believers, go back to the shallow end and walk intentionally with others, teaching them how to move deeper in their relationship with Jesus— teaching them to obey all of His teachings (Matthew 28:20).

Lastly, the third part of this analogy is all about the journey itself. Your life in the pool ultimately represents your life in Christ. You will never walk in the fullness of your freedom unless you get in the pool and make your way to the deep end (with others). On your way, be careful to keep your eyes on Jesus, so you don't drown.

Your journey for the fullness of faith and freedom can begin today. Your Reframe today is not just about freedom for you, but for all those who God seeks to reach through you! Welcome to the journey! Enjoy your new and/or healthier Reframe!

7 MAJOR MILESTONES

PERSONAL SPIRITUAL MARKERS

For a healthy reframe to take place in our lives, there were seven major areas of realignment— we are calling those milestones. Why? Because each of these was a huge hurdle for us. And, they were liberating breakthroughs. So, here they are;

First- "Because I said so" was no longer sufficient.

We grew up in a generation that was learning how to ask questions without being labeled a heretic or rebel. In most adult circles, it was not safe to ask questions that in any way showed areas of consideration in faith development. We didn't see much room for grace regarding these words from the apostle Paul,

> *Philippians 3:15 (ESV) Let those of us who are mature think this way, and if in anything you think otherwise, God will reveal that also to you.*

Just telling people what to believe lacks effectiveness in comparison to allowing them to ask questions and believe God will provide the Truth (in His timing and in His way). Our encouragement is towards allowing people to ask questions, even when it may seem the answer is in plain sight. Remember, what is in plain sight to you now was not always so.

This breakthrough and the spiritual marker is significant. Once we were able to move past the "Because I said so" form of learning and living, we began to experience the Holy Spirit's leading in many different ways. Our love for God and His Word grew exponentially. Our passion for Jesus as The Way, Truth, and Life found its place in our everyday faith and practice.

SECOND- BRIDGING THE GAP BETWEEN THE SACRED AND THE SECULAR BECAME IMPORTANT.

The unfortunate fallout of paid pastors and ministry leaders is the underlying assumption that those people are special above and beyond the people in the pews. In other words, the real world changers and ministers were those on the platform. This would mean that everyone else had been relegated to make a difference in their secular workplaces under the instructions given by the more sacred roles in the local church. Check out these word from the apostle Peter;

> *1 Peter 2:9-10 (AMP) 9 But you are a chosen race, a royal priesthood, a consecrated nation, a [special] people for God's possession, so that you may proclaim the excellencies [the wonderful deeds and virtues and perfections] of Him who called you out of darkness into His marvelous light. 10 Once you were not a people [at all], but now you are God's people; once you had not received mercy, but now you have received mercy.*

Wait! You mean people in the seats carry the same light and Gospel that pastors and church leaders do? Yes! We cannot express in words how freeing and exciting this has been for so many people we've worked with. Of course, we all have different roles and responsibilities, but we are all missionaries, priests, set apart, consecrated— called to come to Him, then be sent by Him with the same message of hope, love, grace, mercy, and salvation!

What new and profound respect we would have for each other in the local church if we appreciated each other's gifts and abilities, calling and anointing, uniqueness and differences, roles and responsibilities. This is a body of believers that has been taught and has believed that it is better to have the sounds of harmony instead of unison. Unison means we all sound the same. Harmony is different notes that sound great together in a single context. Friends, let's bridge the gap between the sacred and secular by coming together and blending our uniquenesses for one sweet sound to our Savior!

THIRD- CHRISTIAN ONE-LINER'S BECAME POWERLESS AND INSUFFICIENT.

"Just trust God." Have you ever been graced with that beautiful and profound piece of wisdom while in the middle of your turmoil or tragedy? It probably didn't provide you the instant peace and joy you were expecting. You see, it's not that the statement is wrong— it's just not complete. It's, well, impersonal and cold.

We spent so many years in ministry where one-liners were the easier, faster, more efficient way of ministering to the masses. These quick conversations were usually directed towards those needing employment, lacking provisions, those who were hurting, the struggling marriage, the stressed, and the depressed.

Again, the advice was not always incorrect. The more significant point is, it was never going to be the answer or the cure. It was never going to replace walking in the messy confusions and chaos of people's lives. Academic approaches were not bettering other's faith to spiritual matters of faith and living. Sometimes, we lacked the attention and care for the hearts of the people because we were too focused on what was mostly behavioral modification.

Loving people with and through their messiness is precisely what God has demonstrated to us throughout His Word. And, it is precisely what we needed when we experienced hurt and trauma in our own lives. In our pain, we noticed how many people began giving us the same one-liners we had dished out all those years. Guess what? They were as you would guess— empty, powerless, and insufficient. Thus began our pursuit of deeper awareness, care, transparency, and authenticity in relationships.

FOURTH- THE PHRASE "WELL, YOU HAVE TO BE CAREFUL WITH THAT" MADE US NAUSEOUS.

We lost count over the years of how many times we heard Christians tell us that we needed to be careful with that. What is "that" that we are to be careful with? Well, it ended up being anything that made them uncomfortable regarding their understanding, knowledge, or experience.

We discovered that any time we started thinking, talking, planning, or operating outside the box, there would always be those who would remind us that we needed to be careful with that. Ugh! We'd love to think they meant well, but when statements like that are made, they're usually made out of fear and insecurity.

As we grow in our relationship with the Lord and become more purposefully and intimately engaged with Kingdom work, we are continually facing the need for changes in our personal paradigms. Growing in knowledge and faith will always require this. You are going to hear from some (out of their fear and faith development) that you need to be careful with that. Our encouragement is not to let that keep you from moving forward in whatever it is God has spoken to you from His Word. If the Holy Spirit has empowered you to go, then go! If what you are doing by following God honors the name of Jesus, then don't be careful, be obedient! Be strong and courageous.

Being careful is the wrong advice— some of the time. It's too easy to put people on the defensive with this kind of advice. More than being careful, we learned to be more attentive. The focus was no longer on being careful (to not make God mad, to not mess up, to not do it wrong, etc.). The goal changed— now it was to listen to God's voice through Scripture, the indwelling Holy Spirit, the wise counsel of trusted friends and family, and testing everything against what we knew God had called us to be and do. Sure, you'll make mistakes, but you'll be far more likely to get up and keep going. Living out of "be careful with that" will almost always keep you bound up and wound up to the point where you are ineffective and unfulfilled.

Fifth - We made the "mistake" of asking the Holy Spirit to wreck our life and ministry.

Years ago, God was doing such great work in our lives to the extent that He was asking us for more. We knew there were areas of our lives that were not wholly surrendered to Him. One of those areas was desiring the supernatural work of the Holy Spirit to transform us entirely. So, what did we do? We asked the Holy Spirit to come and ultimately take over our lives and ministry like never before. We knew it would be messy. However, we had no idea how costly it would be as well.

We knew the fruit of the Spirit. We knew the overall idea about the power of the Holy Spirit. We just hadn't experienced the effect of being fully surrendered to the Holy Spirit. We began to experience the reality of what it means when the power of the Holy Spirit comes on us (Acts 1:8). It changed us as His witnesses in new and exciting ways.

Another significant benefit we began to experience from our reframe was freedom. With the presence of the Holy Spirit increasing more in reality and relevancy, we continued to discover newfound freedoms (2 Corinthians 3:17).

We don't want to repeat what we have already said in an earlier chapter on the Holy Spirit. However, we want to express to you how life-changing it was when we started taking Jesus seriously as He spoke about the work of the Holy Spirit in places like John 16:5-15. Desiring the Holy Spirit to have His rightful place in your life means giving up all other perceived rights over any other area of your life. When you experience this kind of surrender, you will also experience freedom and fulfillment as well as purpose and usefulness in God's Kingdom.

Your experiences (if they are genuine and authentic) with the Holy Spirit will always come from your encounters with Him. Continue to seek the incredible work of the Holy Spirit in your life by allowing Him to stay in charge. When you pray, ask the Holy Spirit to make known to you the more profound things of the heart of God as well as your life's response to the truth of Jesus Christ and His Gospel!

Sixth- Roles and responsibilities surpassed titles and positions.

We spent so many years trying to figure out and live out what we were told our job description was. We lived far too long mixing titles and positions with calling. Here's the deal; you probably already know that the majority of the positions and titles we have in the local church are not found in the Bible. And, even if you could stretch it a little and make some of them work, they certainly aren't fulfilled the same way today as they were two thousand years ago.

This is a follow up to the second major milestone in our breakthrough. When we learned to stop living out a title and job description, we became much more useful to Jesus and His church. We started seeing more and more people step into their calling, roles, anointing, and responsibilities without needing an official title or position in the church. We found out that we were less in the way when we stopped labeling everyone with titles. When we remove the positions and titles that are unable to capture the uniqueness of people's gifs and abilities, we can bless them and released them into their areas of service.

There have been several times in the last several decades that we have not served on a church staff. The perceived threat from this was to our identity as pastors. That title and position was not ours, so what would we become? Who would we be? When we discovered how to live life without labels, we found a whole new dimension to the Christian faith that we never knew before. It was liberating. It was more than refreshing. It gave us the ability to love people, and not try and change them. When it finally sunk in that our job was not to get people to conform, we could release that work to the Holy Spirit and live out the Great Commandment (Luke 10:27) and the Great Commission (Matthew 28:18-20).

When we care about reaching people with the full Gospel (not just for salvation), we invest differently. We operate differently around and with each other. We discover being one body with many parts— none more important than the other!

SEVENTH- TRUSTING AND LOVING GOD WON OVER HELPING AND PERFORMING FOR HIM.

We saved this one for last for a good reason. This is the one that we find ourselves working on continuously. This will continue to be instrumental in our faith development and transformation. This regularly taps into our weaknesses, pride, insecurities, fears, and doubts. A passage of Scripture that has remained foundational for us is a proverb. Here it is,

> *Proverbs 3:5-8 (AMP) 5 Trust in and rely confidently on the Lord with all your heart And do not rely on your own insight or understanding. 6 In all your ways know and acknowledge and recognize Him, and He will make your paths straight and smooth [removing obstacles that block your way]. 7 Do not be wise in your own eyes; Fear the Lord [with reverent awe and obedience] and turn [entirely] away from evil. 8 It will be health to your body [your marrow, your nerves, your sinews, your muscles—all your inner parts] And refreshment (physical well-being) to your bones.*

You can see now why this has to be a daily thing for us. Our initial reaction/response to most anything is from our flesh (our perspective and will). Whether we were trying to do good for Him or merely trying to step in and help Him, we found that we were often placing that above knowing, trusting, and loving Him. The praise here is that if we stop trying to help Him by figuring things out on our merit, wisdom, or insight, we will get to where we need to be. This is often very difficult.

Learning to love Jesus as our Lord and Savior made more sense when we learned just how much He loves us. He will do what is best for us because of His love for us.

No matter where you are in your journey, don't stop. Keep asking questions. Keep growing in your love for God, and you will see just how much you can trust Him. Let this final passage encourage and strengthen you;

> *Psalm 37:5 (ESV) Commit your way to the Lord; trust in Him, and He will act.*

ABOUT THE AUTHORS

Clay and Laura Gatlin have three sons, three grandsons, and family spread all throughout the country.

Clay graduated from Colorado Christian University and Southwestern Baptist Theological Seminary. He started serving as an intern at a local church in Colorado in 1989. From there, he served in denominational as well as nondenominational churches in Colorado, Texas, Alaska, and California. Clay has served churches on staff as a youth pastor, men's pastor, family pastor, executive pastor, teaching pastor, church planter, and lead pastor. He has also served the greater body of Christ as executive director, missions director, life coach and consultant.

Laura has attended Cosumnes River College and Colorado Christian University. Laura has served alongside Clay for over 27 years. Laura is a prolific writer and teacher. She has written devotionals, Bible studies, and sermon series. Laura has spoken at a number of churches and events covering a myriad of topics and themes.

In 2018, Clay and Laura transitioned from their roles at a church in California in order to continue working with churches all over the world. They officially launched Reframe Ministries, Inc., that same year. Clay serves as the president and executive director of Reframe Ministries, Inc. He and Laura also serve as board members for this ministry.